Win or Go Home

*A Guide to Negotiation Success in
Competition and in Life*

Cristina C. Knolton
Southwestern Law School

H. Nyree Gray
Claremont McKenna College

CAROLINA ACADEMIC PRESS
Durham, North Carolina

Copyright © 2017
Carolina Academic Press, LLC
All Rights Reserved

Library of Congress Cataloging-in-Publication Data

Names: Knolton, Cristina C., author. | Gray, H. Nyree.
Title: Win or go home : a guide to negotiation success in competition and in
life / by Cristina C. Knolton and H. Nyree Gray.
Description: Durham, North Carolina : Carolina Academic Press, 2016. |
Includes bibliographical references and index.
Identifiers: LCCN 2016036258 | ISBN 9781611638639 (alk. paper)
Subjects: LCSH: Dispute resolution (Law)--United States. |
Negotiation--United States. | Mediation--United States.
Classification: LCC KF9084 .K66 2016 | DDC 347.73/9--dc23
LC record available at https://lccn.loc.gov/2016036258

CAROLINA ACADEMIC PRESS, LLC
700 Kent Street
Durham, North Carolina 27701
Telephone (919) 489-7486
Fax (919) 493-5668
www.cap-press.com

Printed in the United States of America

Win or Go Home

For Derek, Julia, Ashley, Hailey, Derek Joe,
Natalee, Papa, and Nana
CK

For Jeremy, Jeremiah, Preston, and Mom
NG

For every student that has given us the privilege of
teaching them negotiation
NG and CK

Contents

Acknowledgments

We are grateful to those who read and commented on this book during its many drafts, especially Austen Parrish, Dean of Indiana University Maurer School of Law and James H. Rudy Professor of Law, Paul Bateman, Professor of Legal Analysis, Writing, and Skills at Southwestern Law School, and our research assistant, Ryan Abelman. We are also grateful for the support of Southwestern Law School and our Southwestern students who have inspired many of the techniques we recommend in this book.

About the Authors

Cristina C. Knolton: Professor Knolton is an Associate Professor of Legal Writing, Analysis and Skills at Southwestern Law School, where she teaches contracts, negotiation, legal writing, and legal analysis. Professor Knolton has also taught in the areas of mediation, property, marital property, and bar preparation.

Professor Knolton is currently the co-director of the Negotiation Honors Program. As a part of the program, Professor Knolton teaches Negotiation Honors and coaches Southwestern Law School's national negotiation and alternative dispute resolution teams.

Professor Knolton has spoken before academic and professional forums on topics such as "Negotiation Techniques for Practicing Lawyers," "Negotiation Tactics in Criminal Defense," "A Lawyer's Role as an Advocate in the Legal System," "How to Succeed in Law School," and "Incorporating Exams into the Legal Writing Classroom." Professor Knolton is also the co-author of "Hard Nosed Advice from a Cranky Law Professor: How to Succeed in Law School."

After completing her law degree at the University of Texas, where she was a member of the Texas Law Review, Professor Knolton began her legal career as a real estate attorney at the firm of Akin, Gump, Strauss, Haeur & Feld in San Antonio, Texas, representing commercial real estate clients in the acquisition, sale, ownership, and leasing of income-producing properties. She has also served as a mediator for the Lubbock County Alternative Dispute Resource Center.

H. Nyree Gray: Nyree Gray is the Chief Civil Rights Officer and Title IX coordinator for Claremont McKenna College. Prior to joining Claremont McKenna College, Nyree Gray was an Associate Professor of Law and Dean of Students at Southwestern Law School. Professor Gray has taught in the areas of interviewing, counseling and negotiation, lawyering skills courses, and bar exam success. At Southwestern Law School, Professor Gray served the co-director of the Negotiation Honors Program. The team competes nationally and internationally in various alternative dispute resolution competitions. In addition, Professor Gray was also the co-director of the first ever Hawaii Alternative Dispute Resolution Intersession Program, which provided law students the opportunity to take specialized courses in Negotiation, Mediation, and Conflict Resolution and Entertainment Law courses while cruising.

Prior to her career in higher education, Professor Gray practiced civil litigation and was a member of the law school's adjunct faculty, teaching Interviewing, Counseling and Negotiating and serving on the Faculty Ad Hoc Bar Examination Task Force prior to her full-time appointment. Her areas of practice included contractual litigation, labor and employment law. A "Southern California Super Lawyer Rising Star" (a distinction for lawyers considered in the top 2.5 percent of their practice area), Professor Gray litigated plaintiff employment discrimination claims in the areas of race, age, gender and sexual harassment in both state and federal courts, and successfully argued before the 9th Circuit Court of Appeals. She has been a featured lecturer on employment law, alternative dispute resolution and conflict management at the University of California, Irvine, and the University of California, Riverside.

Introduction

The purpose of this book is to assist students with their preparation for law school negotiation competitions and to provide a resource to anyone who wants to learn about or improve on negotiation techniques and strategies. Our hope is that you will be able to use this book as a resource to assist with your strategy and understanding of the competition process. We also believe it will be a great guide for the law professor and/or generous alum who has graciously agreed to coach students for the first time. Lastly, the approaches and insights we share in this book will assist anyone who wants to learn more about negotiation in general. After all, the techniques set forth in this book work in competition because they reflect effective negotiation techniques in the real practice of law. To that end, let us begin.

Students should be encouraged to participate in competitions. The ability to hone practical skills while in law school has several benefits. Law school is about preparing to enter a profession. Part of the preparation requires lawyering skills and these skills will not be attained by reading and briefing cases alone. Students need opportunities to experience the role of a lawyer advocating for clients and working with opposing counsel. The need for participating in negotiation competitions is supported by an increasing awareness of the importance of negotiation as a core competency skill across the legal curriculum.

Many schools have formal programs and faculty advisors to assist students with their preparation; however, a large number of law schools are still limited to just Moot Court and/or Trial Advocacy programs. Other competitions, such as negotiation, client counseling, and mediation, are often left for students to maneuver on their own. The number of competitions in the area of alternative dispute resolution is steadily increasing, yet the resources available to assist with preparation are limited.

That's where we step in. In this book, we provide strategies and tips based on our own experiences during practice as well as on our experience at various competitions. In addition to our experience in negotiating contracts, leases, and settlement agreements, we have participated in countless numbers of competitions over the years and have had our fair share of judging competitions. Thus, we are able to provide real-world practical advice, as well as the judge's perspective when scoring competitors.

The process and approaches we describe in this book are the same things we share with the members of our own team. These are strategies we have implemented and when executed properly have been successful. At the end of the day, students are encouraged to adjust the styles and techniques to fit their personality and strengths and to highlight their skill set. It is important for each individual to develop a style that feels comfortable and that highlights their individual strengths.

We want to start with a reoccurring theme: HAVE FUN! There are times when you can do everything right but certain things happen beyond your control. You face a crazy team. You have a judge fall asleep. Both of which we have experienced. Just keep in mind the real victory is in the process. Your ability to expand your skill set, gain confidence, and improve your own abilities is its own reward. Yeah, we know ... a trophy doesn't hurt either.

Win or Go Home

Chapter 1

Negotiation Competitions: The Basics

Until recently, the focus of law student competitions has been Moot Court and Trial Advocacy. As Alternative Dispute Resolution (ADR) has become more popular, however, several national competitions have emerged allowing law students to display skills relevant to alternative dispute resolution. Negotiation is one of those skills.

What Is a Negotiation Competition?

In a negotiation competition, students assume the role of lawyers who meet to work out the terms of a deal. Most negotiation competitions follow the same format with slight variations. In the typical competition, a team of two students from one law school sits down at a table across from a team of two students from a different law school. Each team represents a different client with a fictitious legal problem, and the teams negotiate a deal that satisfies both clients' interests.

A few weeks before the competition, both teams are given a set of client facts. The client facts include both general facts and confidential facts. The general facts include all facts that both parties know for the purpose of the negotiation. The confidential facts include secret instructions for the team from their client about the client's desires before settling. A well-written problem will have instructions from the client on each issue to be negotiated. In most situations, the problems are written in a manner that will permit a settlement to be reached. At competition, students typically participate in two negotiation rounds: one in the morning and one in the afternoon. Each negotiation round has three stages. The first stage is the negotiation. During this stage, both teams sit down at a table across from each other and negotiate a deal. During this "negotiation" stage, the judges only observe the students. The judges do not interrupt the negotiation and do not ask questions during the round. At the conclusion of the negotiation stage, both teams leave the room to prepare for the second stage—"self-evaluation." The second stage of the competition is the self-evaluation stage. During the self-evaluation stage, each team reflects on their performance during the negotiation. At this time, the judges are free to ask the students questions about the round. Finally, the round concludes with a "feedback" stage where the judges have an opportunity to provide feedback to the students about their overall performance.

Although all competitors go through these three "stages," not all competitors follow the same steps within each stage. Our recommended steps for each stage follow.

The Negotiation Stage

The negotiation stage is limited to a period of time ranging from thirty minutes to an hour. A typical round is fifty minutes. Within the time period allowed, your task is to negotiate a favorable settlement for your client. In obtaining the settlement, you should follow the steps below.

A. Greeting and Introduction

You should start the negotiation by standing up and introducing yourself to the other team. Each team member should shake the hand of the opposing competitors. At that point, teams tend to take one of two approaches. Some competitors start by doing a little ice breaking prior to getting down to business. This sets a relaxed and cordial environment for the negotiation. Other teams tend to "take the table" immediately to show the judges they are in control of the negotiation.

Ice Breaking. Teams that start with ice-breaking will start with questions like "Did you have trouble finding our office?," "How was traffic?" or "Did you catch the Laker game?" Teams that take this approach most closely reflect the real practice of law. Most attorneys do not walk in the room and begin to discuss their client's case within the first breath. Rather, they take a few minutes to get acquainted and settle in. Thus, some judges will relate to this approach and appreciate the attempt to set a cooperative tone. However, if the opposing team does not play along and actually gets the negotiation rolling, you run the risk the opposing team will gain more attention from the judges.

Taking the Table. The other common approach at the beginning of the round is to "take the table." Under this approach, a team begins the negotiation at the moment the judges say to begin. In fact, many teams race to be the first to speak, hoping it will win the attention of the judges from the start. When taking this approach, remember two things.

First, if you do speak first, make it count. You should have your "introduction" planned prior to the round. Your introduction should include (i) a brief summary of why the parties are at the table; and (ii) a brief summary of your client's interests. This is your first chance to frame the issues in your favor and it is crucial you do not pass up on this opportunity. Your introduction should familiarize the judges with the facts of the negotiation and make the judges believe your client has the stronger position.

Second, don't make yourself look silly trying to speak first. Often teams find it so important to talk first that they end up talking over each other within the first few minutes of the negotiation. Not only does it give a bad impression to the judges, but it will also create a poor tone between the teams and will likely affect the rest of the round. It is not critical to be the first to speak in the negotiation. It is critical to gain control and maintain it. Thus, if the opposing team speaks first, let them talk and be sure to come back with a strong response indicating you also have your client's interests at heart. For more specific tips on creating an effective introduction, see Chapter 4.

B. Information Gathering

The next step in the round is to gather information from your opponent. Not just any information. You must gather information that will ultimately help you later in the bargaining stage of the negotiation. If you are representing the seller in the sale of a house, do not merely ask the buyer's attorneys "What are your interests?" Your opponent will happily tell you that the buyer's interest is to buy the property at a low cost. Not very helpful information. A more useful question would gather information regarding the buyer's current living situation. If you find out whether the buyer currently owns a home and whether the buyer is planning on selling the home, you can use this information as the negotiation progresses. For example, if the buyer is selling his home and has a current offer on his house, he is likely to pay more money for your client's home because he needs to move quickly. If you are lucky enough to get this type of information from the other side, make sure you use it to your advantage later in the negotiation.

Another note. Some information-gathering questions will be more appropriate for the very beginning of the negotiation and others will be more appropriate as you begin to discuss a specific topic. Carefully think about when the question would be best asked. If you are seeking general information that will be helpful throughout the entire negotiation, ask the question up front. If you are seeking information specific to one issue, you may want to hold off until you get to negotiating the specific term.

Although some teams skip the information gathering portion of the negotiation, it is a critical stage and if done correctly can put you one step ahead of the other team.

C. Setting an Agenda

After you have gathered information from the other side, the teams should set an agenda for the negotiation. An agenda is a plan for the meeting indicating what issues will be discussed and the order in which the issues will be discussed. An agenda is necessary to make sure both sides have an understanding of where the negotiation is going and to make sure the negotiation stays organized. Your agenda in a negotiation for the sale of a house might include (i) the price of the home; (ii) the time for closing; and (iii) improvements that must be made to the home before closing.

An agenda has several benefits in a negotiation. Not only does an agenda keep the parties organized, but it gives both sides a chance to evaluate what the opposing side's interests are. Wouldn't you rather know at the beginning of a negotiation exactly what your opponent is seeking? After all, if you know they are going to need several different things, you may not give as much on the first few things they ask for because you know you are going to need to give on additional terms as the negotiation progresses. Knowing at the beginning of the negotiation all the issues that will be addressed will also calm the nerves of everyone at the table. If your opponents know their key issue is on the agenda and is going to be addressed later in the negotiation, they will be able to stop worrying about that issue and focus on the issues that come up first on the agenda.

Your agenda should be concise. Three is a beautiful number. Four is great as well. If your agenda exceeds four issues, it is probably too long. Try to group ideas together to make a manageable number of categories. If the negotiation problem you are working on provides an explicit list of issues to be addressed, use those issues as your agenda.

Don't fight over the agenda. Some teams become so set on their own agenda that if the opposing side presents a different group of items, the teams spend time negotiating what the agenda should be. This is a waste of time. If your opponent sets an agenda and it has the same issues as you want to discuss, great. Rather than trying to put up the same thing in different words, take control of the negotiation by deciding which issue should be discussed first. If you have an additional issue to discuss that is not listed on your opponent's agenda, simply add the additional item to the list.

Stick to the agenda. Too often teams set forth a great agenda at the beginning of the negotiation but then proceed to discuss the issues randomly without any attempt to use the agenda as a guide to when issues will be addressed. If you set an agenda, refer back to it during the negotiation and do your best to keep the negotiation organized by addressing each issue on your agenda in the order originally agreed.

Although setting the agenda can give you control over the negotiation, letting the other side handle this part of the negotiation has its advantages. The opposing side's agenda can give you critical information about their bottom line/interests. For example, if the opposing team lists an item on an agenda that was not of interest to your client, you will know the issue is important to your opponent. If the item is not a critical one for your client, you can leverage it against your opponent to get something you want.

You can find additional tips on setting an agenda and keeping the negotiation organized in Chapter 5.

D. Bargaining

The bargaining stage is the part of the round where the parties actually negotiate the terms of the deal. This part of the negotiation starts by one of the teams making an opening offer. Your job is to get your opponent to move closer to your position. To do this, you have to convince the opposing side that your position is reasonable. You have to justify your offers and force your opponent to make concessions. Easier said than done. Getting the best deal possible for your client requires mastering various techniques. For example, should you make the opening offer? How high should your opening offer be? When should you concede and move off your demands? All of these techniques and more are discussed in Chapter 8.

For now, just remember that your job is to serve your client's interests. In some cases, that may mean you need to be tough and stick close to your opening position. In other cases, it may mean you need to be flexible because your client really needs a deal. Make sure you know what your client's interests are and stay focused on those interests throughout the negotiation.

E. Agreement and Closing

Once both sides have agreed upon the terms of the agreement, you should recap the entire agreement reached by the parties. Often the teams will think they reached an agreement, only to realize they actually have different versions of what agreement was reached. Double check that both teams understand the precise terms agreed to (i.e., summarize the terms) before leaving the table.

Remember to keep track of your time during the round so you have an opportunity to complete this summary. Five minutes should be sufficient to summarize the terms. When there are only ten minutes remaining in the round, you should start winding down the issue you are discussing so you can move into your closing. If you have not agreed upon all the terms discussed, don't worry. Summarize what you have agreed upon and make arrangements for a meeting at a future point. Skilled advocates always end the negotiation on time and are not stopped by the judges because time has expired.

What happens if you don't come to an agreement? Nothing. Often negotiation problems are complex enough that an agreement is difficult to reach. Do your best to agree to as many terms as possible, but avoid rushing into an agreement merely because you are running out of time. Making large jumps in the bargaining process because of time pressure diminishes the hard work you put in throughout the entire negotiation. Leaving a strong impression at the end of the negotiation is better than leaving the judges with the impression you caved at the last minute.

———

Remember, although most good negotiations generally follow the forgoing steps, every negotiation is different. The teams at the table are ultimately in control of what steps are followed. The judges will not regulate the round. If one team takes a different approach, your job is to get the round to follow the path you think is most effective. If your opponent starts the negotiation by making an opening offer without asking any questions or setting an agenda, you should politely tell your opponent that before delving into the terms of the deal you had a few questions you were hoping they could answer. Ultimately, if the round takes an unexpected turn and does not follow the steps set forth above, don't worry. Just keep the negotiation as organized as possible.

The Self-Evaluation Stage

At the completion of the negotiation round, both teams will leave the room to prepare a "self-evaluation." The self-evaluation is an opportunity for students to reflect on their performance during the negotiation. Typically, students are asked to discuss two questions: (i) what parts of the negotiation the students would change if faced with the same situation again; and (ii) how well the students' strategy worked with respect to the outcome reached. Self-evaluations typically last ten minutes per team. Chapter 12 discusses specific tips in creating an effective self-evaluation.

The Feedback Stage

After both teams have completed their self-evaluations, the judges who observed the round will provide feedback to the competitors. At this point, your job is to listen. The judges have spent an hour listening to you speak and this is the judges' opportunity to impart their wisdom on you. Listen to their comments with an open mind. Judges have very insightful tips they picked up from negotiating in practice and their advice is both interesting and helpful.

Occasionally, you will get a judge who provides advice that is not helpful or actually defies all principles of logic. We have had our fair share of those comments. For example, a judge once told us we obtained too much money for our client and suggested that we should have started the negotiation by opening with our bottom line. You do not have to agree with or apply the feedback you receive from the judges. You just have to listen to it. You should never express your disagreement regarding a comment in front of the judges. You should simply smile and nod and then apply whatever feedback you found most helpful in future rounds.

You may also get conflicting advice from judges. For example, one judge may tell your team that it needed more force and power in the negotiation and another judge watching the same round may say your team was too forceful. It happens. Every judge is different and each judge has his or her own experiences with negotiation. Smile and nod. Once you leave the room, decide what advice you want to apply and what advice you want to leave behind. After all, this experience is not far off from the real practice of law where you will often receive different advice from various lawyers and mediators who observe your style of negotiation.

Now you know the basics of what to expect at a negotiation competition. Next we'll provide you tips on how to do well throughout the competition.

Quiz Yourself

1. Which of the following demonstrates the stages of the negotiation in proper order?

    a. Introduction, Agenda, Information Gathering, Bargaining, Agreement and Closing

    b. Introduction, Agenda, Bargaining, Information Gathering, Agreement and Closing

    c. Introduction, Information Gathering, Agenda, Bargaining, Agreement and Closing

    d. Introduction, Bargaining, Information Gathering, Agenda, Agreement and Closing

2. **Name a Pro and Con of the "Ice Breaking" approach?**

   Pro:

   Con:

3. **True or False:** It is critical to be the first to speak in the negotiation.

4. **True or False.** The purpose of asking information gathering questions is to put the opposing side on their heels and make them feel backed into a corner.

5. **Which of the following statements is accurate when setting an agenda?**
   a. Your agenda should be detailed and lengthy.
   b. The more items in your agenda the better.
   c. Using the agenda you prepared is critical to a successful negotiation.
   d. The opposing side's agenda can give you critical information about their interests.

Chapter 2

 ## Choosing a Negotiation Style

One of the biggest decisions you need to make before competing is what style you will use at the competition. Teams use a variety of negotiation styles, but most styles fall in one of two categories: adversarial or cooperative. We recommend taking a blended approach that incorporates the strengths of each style.

The Adversarial Approach

Adversarial negotiators generally start the bidding process with high offers, make minimal concessions, and conceal information. Adversarial negotiators often use various psychological games, such as anger, intimidation, and threats to get what they want. Some of the toughest rounds we have seen have been against teams who used an adversarial approach. We have faced teams who absolutely refused to move from their initial offer. We have faced teams who yelled and screamed at our students. We have faced teams who used ploys and techniques to try to curry favor with the judges. How to respond to these challenges is discussed in Chapter 9 of this book.

Using the adversarial approach can be effective. If you have judges who use an adversarial approach in their law practice, they will think the round is brilliant and will likely score your team well. You may also appear to be the team in control of the negotiation. You can certainly win some negotiation competitions using this approach. However, there are several downsides to the adversarial approach as well. First, the adversarial approach tends to create a rift between the parties. It causes the opposing counsel to dislike each other. When someone dislikes you, they are less likely to give you what you want. Furthermore, using the adversarial approach makes it more difficult to find the settlement zone. If one side starts with a high offer and makes few concessions, the opposing side is likely to do the same. The result is two parties who are far away from reaching a deal.

Most judges are not fond of the adversarial approach. On numerous occasions we have heard judges tell adversarial teams that their strategy disserved their client's interests. For example, if a team starts with an extraordinarily high opening offer and the team is inflexible with the terms of the deal, the team is unlikely to reach an agreement. Those teams will not be serving the interests of a client who really wanted to avoid litigation. The blame will fall on the adversarial team who acted unreasonably. Thus, this approach is a risky one. It could turn out well, but more often than not it will end with your team going home.

The Cooperative Approach

Cooperative negotiators start with a reasonable offer, make concessions easily, and are forthcoming with information. Cooperative negotiators seek to find an agreement that works well for both sides. Their focus is to get a deal (rather than to get the best deal possible). Cooperative negotiators are problem solvers who are at the table to find a way to make both parties happy.

The cooperative approach can be effective. The cooperative approach tends to help build rapport between the teams. This rapport can ultimately help the parties reach agreement. The cooperative approach is also effective because it makes the settlement zone easier to find. If both parties are making reasonable offers, they are much more likely to find a number or deal that works for both parties. If your client's interest is to reach a deal, the cooperative approach is one way of helping reach that goal.

The cooperative approach is the trend in the modern world of negotiation. Most negotiation problems are written so that reaching an agreement is critical to both sides and using a cooperative approach is the best way to be sure you reach an agreement.

Problems arise, however, if the negotiators put too much focus on cooperation and too little focus on serving their client's interests. Take the following example. Derek sues his employer for wrongful termination. He tells you he hopes to receive $50,000 in damages, but is ultimately willing to settle for any amount offered rather than pursue litigation because he has recently accepted a new position and does not want his new employer to find out he was terminated. If your sole focus is on reaching an agreement, your offers may drop too quickly. Perhaps you settle for $10,000. Many judges will appreciate your flexibility and applaud your team for reaching a deal favorable for your client. However, if the next team comes in and negotiates $30,000 and a confidentiality clause, the judges are likely to appreciate that negotiation more. Thus, you have to be careful not to be too accommodating. You cannot be so cooperative that you leave money or terms on the table that you could have brought back to your client. You have to test the waters, see what you can get, and ultimately go home with not just any deal, but the best deal available.

Our Recommendation: The Blended Approach

Which of the two negotiation strategies should you use in competition? Our advice is to create your own blend. Instead of being an adversarial negotiator or a cooperative negotiator, you should create a mold of the two approaches that works with your personality. If you are generally more aggressive, keep in mind the importance of being flexible and finding the settlement zone. If you tend to be a pushover, remember to hold strong and try to get as much for your client as possible. The important thing is to be balanced. We advise our students to take a blended approach. You don't want to be so firm in trying to get terms favorable for your client that you fail to find an agreement. You also don't want to be so flexible that you miss opportunities to bring back favorable terms to your client. Here are a few tips:

A. Start Reasonably High Rather Than Extraordinarily High

You don't want your opening offer to be unreasonable. If your opponent thinks you are unreasonable, they will be unreasonable in return, and your offers will be too far apart to find the settlement zone. You will also lose credibility because you will be forced to make large concessions to come down to the settlement zone.

On the other hand, you also don't want to start the negotiation at your bottom line. You need to leave room for movement and you need to demonstrate for the judges that you tried to get a favorable deal for your client.

A good rule of thumb is to start a little above what your ideal agreement would be. In Derek's situation, $60,000 would be a reasonable starting point knowing you ideally wanted to get $50,000. An opening of $70,000 would also be a good starting spot. Starting at $100,000 is probably too high, especially given that you could have to settle for as little as $10,000. Similarly, starting at $30,000 is too low given that Derek would ideally like $50,000.

Think big, but be reasonable.

B. Make Small Concessions Often Rather Than Large Concessions Seldom

If you only make a few concessions during a round, they will have to be big and you will lose your opportunity to see if you can achieve something in the middle. For example, if you start at $60,000 and drop to $20,000, you will lose your chance to see if you could have received $40,000. Instead, be forthcoming with your concessions, but make them small. Move from $60,000 to $50,000 to $40,000 to $35,000 to $32,000. This allows you to test the waters and achieve the most favorable terms for your client.

Keep in mind concessions come in forms other than the price. Let's take the purchase of a home as an example. In addition to negotiating the price of the home, you will also need to negotiate ancillary terms. How long does the buyer have to inspect the property? When is the closing date? When will the Seller turn the property over to the buyer? Who is responsible for repairs? What if the Buyer's financing fails? Use these other terms to your advantage when making concessions. Perhaps concede on one of these terms instead of the price. Perhaps when conceding on the price, link it to one of these other terms to make sure you get what you need on that term.

C. Be Firm When It Matters

Part of finding the right balance is to know when to be firm and hold your ground and when to be flexible. For example, don't be firm in setting the agenda (unless the order of the issues really matters). Save your fight for the term your client values most. If there is a whiteboard in the room, don't fight over how the board will be used. Rather, save your firmness for when you really need to encourage the opposing side to make an offer. Be reasonable on the issues that matter least to your client. Be firm on the terms that are the most important.

D. Speak with Confidence, but Be Friendly

You want the judges to think you are in control of the negotiation and the tone in your voice can often make a difference. You should speak firmly and with confidence. However, you also must be likeable. Arrogance is often mistaken for confidence. Be careful which you are portraying. Smile often. Be cordial to the other side. Listen to their ideas and solutions. Be confident, but make sure the judges like you. The same is true in practice. People rarely give money to rude people. Your personality can be a strength or a weakness.

Consider Your Location

In creating the perfect blend of the adversarial and cooperative approaches, think about where you will be competing. Although most judges prefer a cooperative team serving their client's interests to an adversarial team who has lost sight of their client's goals, the amount of cooperation preferred will vary depending on where you are negotiating. In Virginia, for example, we have found judges prefer a slightly more aggressive style, perhaps because those judges use a more aggressive negotiation style in the fast-paced legal community on the east coast. In Canada, judges generally prefer a cooperative style. In fact, from our experience, it is difficult to be too cooperative in Canada. Other states fall somewhere in the middle. Judges in Oregon, for example, prefer the cooperative approach, but not to the same extent as the judges in Canada. California judges tend to prefer aggressive negotiators, but not to the same extent as judges in Virginia. The culture of the judges at a negotiation competition is subject to change over time as the culture of the legal field changes in the area. Think about the legal culture of where you are negotiating as you develop your own negotiation style.

Quiz Yourself

1. **True or False:** One advantage to the adversarial approach is that it increases the likelihood of reaching agreement.

2. **Which of the following are benefits of the cooperative approach (circle all that apply)?**

    a. The cooperative approach makes it easier to find the settlement zone.

    b. The cooperative approach is more likely to build rapport between the parties.

    c. The cooperative approach tends to result in maximum gain for your client.

3. **True or False.** You must follow either a cooperative approach or an adversarial approach. There is little room in between.

4. Your client was injured in a car accident and is suing for personal injury damages. Your client is hoping to receive $30,000, but is willing to settle for as little as $20,000. You estimate the damages are in the $20,000–$30,000 range. Which of the following is the best starting offer?

   a. $80,000

   b. $40,000

   c. $30,000

   d. $20,000

5. **True or False:** When making concessions, it is better to make a lot of smaller concessions, rather than a few larger concessions.

Chapter 3

Know Your Facts

The foundation for any negotiation competition: preparation. What is the first step to preparing? Knowing the facts of the problem you are given. You can adapt your strategy. You can set your own agenda. You can ask whatever information gathering questions you like. You cannot, under any circumstances, change the facts. You cannot exaggerate the facts. You cannot ignore the facts. You cannot make up new facts. You are stuck with the facts you are given and you must make the most of them.

Never Misrepresent Facts

Regardless of what you have seen on television or heard about the practice of law, you may not bend the facts in a negotiation competition. As a general rule of thumb, most lawyers know they are not permitted to provide false information to their opponent. However, most attorneys feel comfortable with a little "bluffing." After all, it is a negotiation, right? That's what negotiators do. They bluff. They lie. They slightly exaggerate. Not in competition. In competition you must stick closely to the facts provided and be careful not to misrepresent any of your facts to the opposing side—including your bottom line. Failure to do so could result in disqualification and will almost certainly result in a low score.

Does that mean you must tell your opponent all facts that weaken your arguments? Certainly not. You have no obligation to disclose negative facts to your opponent. For example, if your confidential facts tell you that your client has five previous convictions for driving under the influence, you are not obligated to tell your opponent. If your opponent asks you about your client's prior criminal record, however, you cannot say it is clean.

If and when to disclose negative facts will be part of your strategy. Trying to keep a negative fact hidden is one effective approach. You can try to avoid any questions that bring the fact into light. That's easier said than done when facing a good team. A good team will ask good information gathering questions and leave you in a position where you have no choice but to disclose the negative information. Another strategy might be to bring in a negative fact yourself so you can shed the best light on the fact and preemptively "take out the sting." Offering a fact yourself shows you are not scared of the fact and the fact will appear less damaging than if you tried to hide the fact but are ultimately required to disclose it.

Let's take an example based on an ABA negotiation problem we have negotiated in the past. Assume you represent a trucking company. The company is being sued because its employee was under the influence of drugs when he crashed the company truck into a building. You know that your client investigated the employee prior to hiring the employee. You also know that during the investigation, your client discovered rumors that the employee had taken illegal substances in the past. Upon further investigation, however, your client confirmed the rumors were not true and thus hired the employee as a driver. You now must deal with the fact that your client had some form of notice of the drug use prior to the accident.

One approach to dealing with this "bad fact" is to try to hide the fact. Simply never bring it up and dodge any questions that lead to that information. The danger in this strategy is that it is dependent on the competence of your opponent. If you can tell that your opponent is not asking questions and has no interest in finding out relevant details of the case, by all means, keep the fact a secret. If your opponent is a good negotiator, however, your opponent will ask the right questions to make sure you disclose the information. If you try to avoid disclosing the information, but ultimately are forced to disclose it, the fact looks worse because you were trying so hard to hide it.

How do you avoid this? Disclose it immediately the first time you are asked. If you openly disclose the fact and frame it in a manner favorable to your client, it will be less damaging. So, if your opponent asks if your client had any knowledge regarding the employee's drug use in the past, you can simply respond:

"No. That is why we are so shocked by what has happened. At the time our client decided to hire the employee, it heard a rumor regarding the employee's prior drug use and did a thorough investigation to be sure there was no sign of drug use. The company was able to confirm the rumor was false and since that day the employee has been a model employee. He is on time every day. He never takes off time. He is responsible. He has been the employee everyone has looked up to in the office."

By taking this strategy, you have taken the negative fact and put a positive spin on it. Openly discussing the fact as though it is not harmful actually diminishes the importance of it. Remember to quickly move on from that topic after you have answered the question. Your answer should end in some sort of movement—either an offer or a question for the other side. Do not leave time for your opponent to think about your answer.

Bottom line: think about negative facts as much as or more than you think about the facts in your favor. Come up with a strategy as to how to deal with those facts. Never lie about those facts. Misrepresenting facts to your opponent is your quickest ticket home.

Avoid Adding Self-Serving Facts

Most negotiation competitions operate under a closed universe. The facts generally supply the competitors with all information necessary to solve the problem. However, the typical fact pattern will end with something like "You may add any facts that are not self-serving." What facts are those? It is difficult to think of a fact you would want to add that does not help you in some way. Chances are if you want to include the fact it is because it bolsters your argument or puts you in a stronger position. If it does, you cannot include it. "You may add any facts that are not self-serving" is really just code for "Don't add any facts at all."

This is not to say that you cannot take a few liberties with your interpretation of facts, but you must limit your interpretations to things that are generally accepted by a majority of the public as true without having to do additional research. For example, making the statement California has sunny weather is generally true and most people would accept it as true without having to Google it. On the other hand, saying "Last year, on August 12, the temperature was 102 degrees," would exceed your leeway with the facts.

Sometimes bringing in real world comparisons makes the negotiation more interesting. It keeps your judges tuned into your channel. Perhaps you compare your client's basketball ability to LeBron James' abilities. Maybe you compare your client's new electronic store to Apple. This is very different from creating a self-serving fact. A self-serving fact is one that is not provided in your general or confidential facts and could not be reasonably inferred from common knowledge or competition materials. Creating self-serving facts is an ethical violation in most competitions and usually a basis upon which a team could be disqualified.

If disqualification is not enough incentive, there is another reason not to create new facts. When you include facts that are not in the fact pattern provided, you risk throwing off the rhythm of the problem. Each problem is designed to give balanced arguments for both sides. This creates the motivation for both parties to settle and avoid litigation. Self-serving facts remove the balance and can derail the negotiation. Furthermore, your opposing counsel will not have the ability to respond to your invented facts. Opposing counsel has been given all the tools necessary to respond to facts provided in the problem. Once you inject new facts into the problem, you risk impacting their perception of what is possible and risk losing the deal.

Note: the creation of new facts is different from making inferences based on common knowledge. Always use your common sense in a negotiation. General principles that are reasonably accessible to both sides are acceptable to use in the negotiation. A fact that the other side would have to look up is most likely not an inference, but instead a self-serving fact.

Interpret Confusing Facts in Your Favor

What do you do when you have a fact that can be interpreted in two ways? Interpret the fact given in the light most favorable to your client. As you go through this process, take the time to really think about the problem and what was intended by the author. Decide objectively how you think the judges would interpret the fact given its context among all the other facts in the problem. If it is still unclear what the author meant, use the interpretation that is more favorable for you.

A good rule of thumb in interpreting facts is as follows: if you can sell your interpretation of the facts to the judges in self-evaluation, go with it. If, on the other hand, you think the judges would laugh when they heard your interpretation of the facts, re-think your interpretation. You should use the most favorable interpretation you think an objective judge would agree with.

Never Exceed Your Client's Authority

As you prepare for the negotiation, take time to carefully read your client's instructions. Pay close attention to the words used to reference your client's terms and conditions. This key wording is usually in your confidential instructions. The instructions often trigger phrases to let you know the client's limits. You may see the following term:

Ms. Stone will accept no less than $10,000.

The above phrase should be interpreted as Ms. Stone's bottom line on this issue. The phrase "no less than" is language of limitation and should be construed as the client's desire not to go below the said amount. It does not matter if the opposing side offers $9,999.00. You cannot decide on your own the offer is close enough and accept the deal. You must adhere to what the client proscribes. This phrase is to be distinguished from the following:

Ms. Stone would like $10,000.

The first phrase indicated an absolute condition. The above phrase is a desired outcome, but not an absolute. The phrase "would like" means the client would hope it could happen but understands it may not happen.

Once you receive your confidential instructions, take the time to map out your client's ideal agreement and bottom line for each issue. You should know the maximum your client desires, what amount or condition would be acceptable to your client, and what your client's absolute bottom line is. Failure to adhere to your client's bottom line could alone be enough to prevent you from advancing in the competition. Furthermore, understanding your limits and having a plan about what your client expects allows you and your partner to be consistent with offers and counteroffers.

Avoid Consuming Yourself with Outside Research

Although the fact patterns generally provide you all the information needed for the negotiation, there will be times when the subject matter of the problem is so foreign you find yourself questioning why you ever agreed to compete in the first place. Perhaps you are competing in an entertainment law negotiation competition and you know nothing about how television production companies operate. Maybe you are competing in an environmental negotiation competition and you have never taken a course in environmental law or heard about the impact a recycling facility can have on an eco-conscious coastal community. Don't panic!

Every negotiation competition has a theme (e.g., sports law, environmental law, business transactions, etc.). You do not need to know everything about the area of law to do well. Changes in the legal theme do not change the process of how you negotiate. You should never shy away from a competition just because you are unfamiliar with the subject matter.

Instead of panicking and backing out of the competition, simply do a bit of background research about the area of law at issue. Note, when we say "bit," we mean "bit." In other words, a small amount, a quick search—not a study of the subject matter. You want to do enough research so you are familiar with the overall concepts, but you do not want to delve into the subject matter so deeply that you overthink the problem.

Too much research overrides your ability to come to a deal. If you base your creative solutions on the research you have performed outside the given facts, you run the risk that the other side has not done the same research and is not even remotely familiar with your research. This causes confusion, disorganization, and disaster. After all, you cannot have a conversation with someone who knows nothing about what you are discussing. Furthermore, your opponent can only agree to what has been given to them in the fact pattern. Thus, if your creative solution is based on information outside that fact pattern, your opponent will not have the authority to settle on the solution you provided.

Remember, negotiation competitions tend to have closed universe problems, which means all you need to resolve the problem is contained in the information provided. You should research any language contained in the information provided that you don't understand, but avoid doing so much research that you start to drift away from the instructions given to you by your client. Use your confidential facts as your guide.

The exception to this rule is the limited number of competitions that encourage outside research. If the competition encourages outside research, make sure you understand the acceptable sources for the research. They may limit your search to information that is readily available on the internet or limit your research to only certain websites. As a general rule if you find you and your partner up late studying the Magna Carta, you have probably gone too far. Competitors who get so caught up in research usually fail to focus on the facts provided.

Since we are discussing research, it is important to share one cautionary tale. Please be aware of the opposing party who has done too much outside research: the poor saps that did not have the benefit of reading this book and come to the negotiation with a complete PowerPoint of foolishness. You will know it when you see it. Your first impulse will be to just lose your mind and, trust us, we don't blame you. Before you lose your cool, take a breath. Whatever they are saying simply doesn't matter. Don't be rude. Don't pick a fight. Allow them a minute to get out their point (but only a minute … literally), then simply say: "that is very interesting, but today we really need to focus on the following" (and then insert your agenda). This approach shows the judges that you are not scared of the other side's information and not bothered by their approach. It also sends the message that your opponent's research is irrelevant without having to state it bluntly.

Quiz Yourself

1. **True or False.** In competition, "bluffing" as to your bottom line is acceptable.

2. **True or False.** You are not obligated to disclose negative facts to your opponent.

3. **When faced with an ambiguous fact, you should:**

    a. Call the competition administrator immediately to get clarification.

    b. Stop practicing until someone provides further clarification on the ambiguous fact.

    c. Drive yourself crazy trying to make the fact make sense.

    d. Interpret the fact in the light most favorable to your client and move on.

4. **Which of the following sets forth a bottom line for your client?**

   a. Ms. Joy will pay no more than $50,000.

   b. Ms. Joy would like to pay $50,000.

   c. Ms. Joy's goal is to pay $50,000

5. **True or False.** Performing extensive outside research is a good technique to get an extra edge over your opponent.

Chapter 4

 **Creating an Effective Introduction**

Your job in every negotiation: get your opponent to see the facts from your client's perspective. Whether you are the first to speak during a negotiation is far less important than the content that comes out of your mouth when you do speak. People tend to get caught up on "taking the table" and getting control over the negotiation by talking before their opponent does. These people tend to be so focused on speaking first that they lose sight of the real purpose of an introduction and forget how important the content of what they say is to their negotiation success.

Frame the Issues Persuasively

Your introduction is one of the most critical parts of any negotiation. It is your chance to set the stage; your opportunity to let your opponent see the facts through your client's eyes. The introduction is where you have your biggest opportunity to frame the issues favorably for your side.

Take the following example based on a previous ABA Negotiation problem.

Judy went into the hospital to have nose surgery to look beautiful on her wedding day. Things went terribly wrong during the procedure and Judy ended up in a coma on life support. The three doctors that initially evaluated Judy suggest she is not going to come out of her coma.

Josh, Judy's fiancé, desperately wants to get other neurological experts in to evaluate Judy and try everything they can to save Judy's life. He is hoping that several different doctors will come evaluate Judy, and he would like Judy to stay on life support until all doctors have confirmed there is no chance of revival.

Jim and Susan, Judy's parents, don't feel the same. Although devastated by the loss of their daughter, they have faced reality that Judy has no chance of recovering. Three doctors have already evaluated Judy and all agreed that she will never wake up from her coma. Jim and Susan plan to take Judy off of life support immediately. That is where the negotiation starts. Josh has hired lawyers to negotiate with the parents' lawyers to find a mutually acceptable arrangement for Judy.

Imagine this. Josh's lawyers start the negotiation with a strong introduction. They talk about how much Josh loves Judy. They talk about how Judy was a physical therapist and believed in recovery. They appeal to emotion and emphasize that Judy is entitled to every chance there is at recovery, regardless of how small. That's all Josh wants—"a chance for Judy to recover."

At this point, the parents look heartless. Josh's lawyers have made it sound so reasonable to simply have a few doctors confirm that Judy will not recover. How harmless is that given someone's life is on the line? Why shouldn't we take every precaution before ending someone's life? If the parents' lawyer does not have an effective introduction, the entire negotiation will be conducted under the lens of Josh's point of view and each offer will be made with the "feeling" that Judy deserves every chance to live. The parents' lawyer is likely to feel guilty for rejecting offers that allow doctors to see Judy. The parents' lawyer will feel unreasonable to prevent Judy from having that chance at life.

The lawyer for Judy's parents needs to change the tone. That lawyer's job is to put on a new lens that the negotiation can operate under. Let everyone see the issues from a different point of view. Instead of going along with your opponent's theme for the negotiation, reframe the issues so that there is a more persuasive theme for your client. Maybe something along these lines:

"It is unfortunate that we are forced to meet under these circumstances. Jim and Susan care deeply for Josh and know he is having just as hard a time dealing with Judy's condition as they are. They understand that it is hard to let go and want to hold on to Judy too. However, Jim and Susan have been able to face the hard truth that Judy has no chance of recovery and they are concerned that continuing treatment will only turn Judy into a medical experiment. Judy has already been in the hospital for weeks, prodded and poked by doctor after doctor. In fact, all doctors that have evaluated Judy have confirmed she has no chance of survival. Jim and Susan are concerned that if we continue treatment, their daughter will turn into nothing more than a medical experiment for doctors to try their theories on. The parents care too deeply for Judy to let her become a medical experiment."

By including this introduction, the parents' lawyers have reframed the negotiation. Now every time the other side asks for an additional doctor to see Judy, it not is not about giving Judy hope; rather, it is about how each doctor turns Judy into a bigger science experiment. The experiment theme is a much more favorable light to negotiate the issues under if you represent Jim and Susan.

A strong introduction gives you power. It gives you leverage. It helps your opposing side understand where you are coming from and almost always results in better offers from your opponent.

Create a Structure for Your Introduction

So now you (hopefully) understand the point of the introduction and the value it serves in the negotiation. So how so you create one? A few things you want to always in include:

First, introduce yourself and who you represent.

Second, summarize the facts of the negotiation in a favorable way for your side. Start by thinking about what your theme for the negotiation will be. Is it to give Judy every chance possible? Is it that you must avoid Judy becoming a medical experiment? As you summarize the facts, incorporate your theme as much as possible. By the time you are done with the introduction, your theme should be clear and someone who has not read the problem should be able to understand what the issues are and what the negotiation is about. At the end of your negotiation, anyone listening to the negotiation should understand your client's perspective and will hopefully want your client to prevail.

Third, try to have both you and your partner speak during the introduction. Break up the introduction so that each of you have a part to say. You want to come off as a dynamic duo, not as a dominant and weaker combination.

Fourth, keep it simple. The entire introduction should not be more than two or three minutes. You will lose your punch and effect if you speak for too long or if the opposing side needs to interrupt you.

End Your Introduction with Information-Gathering Questions

Framing the negotiation from your perspective gives you an advantage. You want to maintain that advantage, so do your best to prevent your opposing counsel from framing the negotiation differently. When you finish your introduction, do not sit quietly and leave the table silent for opposing counsel to respond. Opposing counsel is likely to respond with their own version of the events. To avoid this, end your introduction with an information-gathering question so opposing counsel feels obligated to respond. Hopefully this will get the negotiation moving forward without the opposing counsel's theme lingering in the air.

Quiz Yourself

1. **True or False.** It is critical to be the first person to speak at the negotiation table.

2. **Which of the following is the most important aspect of a good introduction?**
   a. It frames the issues favorably for your client.
   b. It allows you to speak first so the judges think you have control of the table.
   c. It shows the judges how clearly and confidently you speak.
   d. It makes opposing counsel scared to negotiate with you.

3. **True or False.** An introduction should be a minimum of three minutes so it takes up significant time in the negotiation and shows your control over what is going to be said at the table.

4. **True or False.** You and your partner should both speak during the introduction.

5. **How can you avoid having the opposing side respond to your introduction with their own framing of the facts?**

Chapter 5

Keeping the Negotiation Organized

Have you ever been watching a movie but turned the channel because you couldn't figure out what was happening? Watching a negotiation competition is like performing a scene from a movie for the judges. Judges want to be involved and entertained from the moment they tune in. A disorganized negotiation causes the judges to tune out and score both teams poorly. One of the most important aspects to an effective negotiation is to keep the negotiation organized. The round should be so organized that the judges can actually anticipate what will happen next. Sometimes this is easier said than done, so allow us to give you some suggestions on how to keep the round in order.

Use an Agenda to Keep Issues in Order

A negotiation should start with an introduction of the parties and transition into info-gathering questions. After both parties are done asking questions, the information obtained should flow into an agenda for the meeting. An agenda is just a quick summary of the issues you want to negotiate and the order in which the issues will be tackled. Teams usually have three to four key areas they need to address.

A. Creating the Agenda

You should use the information obtained during the introduction and information gathering stages to identify what issues should be put on the agenda. After each side has presented their client's concerns, there will likely be some common areas of interests. Start by including those issues on the agenda. Then add any additional points that you need to address that were not covered by the points already set forth. Your agenda may look something like this:

1. Length of the contract;
2. Compensation; and
3. Behavior Clause.

It is important to set the structure of the negotiation very early in the round so the judges can see where the parties are headed. Judges are given all of the information for the negotiation prior to the round. They have the general facts and both sides' confidential facts. They are anticipating the round will go in a certain direction. A good agenda sends a signal to the judges that you understood the problem and have effectively identified the issues that need to be addressed. The agenda also allows both teams to relax and work together because both sides know all of their concerns will ultimately be discussed and they know ahead of time in what order they will be discussed.

B. Follow the Agenda You Set Forth

The next bit of advice seems obvious, but it is one of the most common errors in a negotiation: once you set an agenda, you have to follow it. Setting an agenda loses all of its value if you fail to adhere to the schedule. Often students will set a beautiful agenda and start off right on track by talking about issue one. Students then forget to stay focused on issue one. One team will bring up a great argument and the opposing team will respond with an argument that really relates to item three on the agenda. Now the teams will be talking about item three without ever finishing or summarizing where they were on item one. In the middle of talking about item three, someone will bring up something about item two. Now the teams will be talking about items two and three at the same time. Soon enough all issues will be discussed together. Can you start to feel the chaos? The judges will. In fact, the judges will quickly turn the channel and start thinking about the next show.

Often the most effective person at the table is not the one who has quick comebacks or brilliant justifications. The most effective negotiator tends to be the one who can keep the negotiation organized and keep everyone moving in the right direction.

C. Avoid Negotiating the Agenda

Another common error made in a negotiation: negotiating the issues on the agenda. After reading this book, you will be well trained. You will think about your negotiation problem ahead of time. You will have a perfectly developed agenda that will blow the judges away. The problem is the other side will also have read this book (or at least we hope so). They will have thought about their negotiation problem. They will have developed what they think is a perfect agenda. Their agenda will be different than yours. This is not a time to panic. You are flexible. You are adaptable. You can make anything work.

If your opponent sets forth a different agenda than what you had in mind, do not force your agenda on the group. If your opponent's agenda is missing an item you need to discuss, simply add your item to the agenda. If your opponent's agenda includes all the ideas you need to discuss but in a different order, simply tell the other side you need to discuss the items in a different order. Hopefully it can be resolved that easily. If the opposing team insists on their order, don't waste time fighting about it. Simply start with the issue your opponent wants to start with and transition from that issue into the one you need to discuss within a few minutes.

For example, assume the opposing team lists the agenda set forth above (length, compensation, behavior clause). Perhaps your authority to settle on the length of the contract depends on how much compensation the parties agree to. You may tell your opponent that the agenda set forth looks great, but that you need to discuss compensation first because the other terms of the contract depend on that number. If they agree, you have shown the judges your ability to work together and have preserved the order you wanted. If the other side demands length be discussed first, do not panic and just go with the flow. Agree to discuss length first. As soon as you get into a discussion on length and your opponent gives you a number, tell them that your counter-offer will depend on what they can do on compensation and transition into that issue. Even though compensation was number two on the agenda, you will ultimately end up putting issue one on hold and discussing compensation before reaching an agreement on length. You will look cooperative and in control of the negotiation.

Never lose focus on the purpose of the agenda. It is a tool to keep the parties on the same page so the negotiation stays organized. If you fight over what issues are going to be discussed, you will never be on the same page and it will show throughout the negotiation.

Prioritize Issues

The utility of the agenda is derived from the order that you choose to address the issues. Therefore, the order in which you list items in your agenda takes careful thought. How do you decide which issues are best to discuss first? Here are our tips.

A. Put Dependent Issues Last

Often you will have one or two terms in a negotiation that are dependent on what agreement is reached on a different term. Put the dependent terms last. If the term of years for the contract is directly dependent on how much compensation you are able to achieve, it makes no sense to discuss the term of years first. Put compensation on the agenda before term of years because you know you will not be able to provide helpful offers on the term without first knowing the compensation.

B. Put Your Client's Interests First

Prioritize issues according to what is most important to your client. Fifty minutes goes fast. Even an hour round flies by before you know it. You will start the negotiation thinking you have time to address all of the issues. Something will take longer than you think. You will either fail to discuss certain issues all together, or some of the issues that come up late on the agenda will be given little time for discussion. If you put the most critical issues for your client first, you guarantee that the crucial aspects of the deal will be effectively negotiated in the limited time frame. The concept is similar to taking exams. If you run out of time, you want the quick discussion of an issue to be on the minor issues as opposed to one of the critical issues of the exam.

C. Exception: Save Money (and Other Contentious Issues) for Last

A good rule of thumb is to save money issues to discuss after you have discussed non-monetary issues. I know what you are thinking. What is more important than money? Shouldn't that be first on my list? According to our previous tip—yes! However, slow down and think about what the discussion over money will look like. What do most people fight about? What causes the most tension? Money. As a result, it causes the most strain between the teams and results in the biggest time-suck in any negotiation. Starting with something so adversarial will set a bad tone for the entire round.

Often the better strategy is to discuss non-monetary issues first. Try to find an issue that will build rapport with the other team. If both teams are able to work together on one issue and come up with an agreement that both sides are happy with, it will build momentum for the rest of the round. Hopefully it will be enough momentum that when you do address financial issues it will be smoother.

Another great reason to save money for last: money is a great leveraging tool. A negotiation is about leveraging your strengths. If you have settled on money early in the negotiation, you have less flexibility in other areas because your opponent already got what they wanted on the money. If you hold out, you can leverage more for your client as you give the opposing side the money they need.

Keep these tips in mind when other contentious issues arise as well. Just as it is helpful to build momentum before discussing money, it is equally as helpful to build momentum before discussing contentious issues that are likely to derail the negotiation. Start with something that will help the teams build rapport. Thus, when the contentious issue arises, you are both eager to work together to get the deal done.

There are a lot of good reasons to save difficult issues for last. But remember, if you save these issues for last, save time to get to them!

Feel Comfortable Leveraging Issues

A good negotiator is able to leverage the issues against each other. Don't feel that good organization requires completing one item on the agenda at a time. Often the movement in one area is contingent upon the movement in another. Look for the opportunity to link the resolution of issues together. Assume the parties are negotiating over an employment agreement. One side wants a long term contract and is willing to accept a lower wage to get it. The other side wants a short term contract for more money. A good solution would be to work with both the term and the money together. The flexibility in one area can create the opportunity to make adjustments in the other area.

Negotiating two or more items at once can cause confusion if not well organized. Remember to clearly state your offers. Also think about whether the use of a whiteboard can help keep the negotiation in order. If you see the negotiation becoming unclear, take a step back and restate what the offer for each term is. Make sure if you are attempting to tie issues together, that you are receiving offers from opposing counsel in the same manner. If you offer a certain number of years for a certain amount of money, opposing counsel should give you an offer for each term as well.

Summarize. Summarize. Summarize.

Once you start using all of your tools and discussing multiple issues, your ability to summarize will be crucial to keeping the negotiation organized. Don't wait to summarize at the end of the negotiation. You must summarize as the negotiation progresses, especially as you move from one issue to another. You must then summarize again at the end of the round.

First, you want to take the opportunity to reach a meeting of the minds with the opposing side at the conclusion of each issue. Throughout the negotiation, people will throw numbers around, make offers, make counteroffers, as well as throw out other terms and conditions. It is very easy to lose track of where you are. If you just take a minute to summarize where you are during the discussion of a complex issue, or at a minimum before moving to the next issue, it will allow everyone to stay on the same page. Summarizing during the negotiation makes your team look confident to the judges. Those that summarize and have a sense of where the negotiation is are the ones who appear to be in control of the negotiation.

Second, you must summarize at the end of the entire negotiation. When the teams have reached an agreement on all issues, do a "big summary" of all issues at the end of the round. Include any details the teams have agreed upon. Try to save enough time to fix any disagreements because it is common for one of the teams to have a different idea as to what was agreed upon.

Finally, a summary at the end of the negotiation is necessary even if you don't reach an agreement. Assume there are five minutes left in the round and you haven't completely resolved all items on the agenda. It is far better to spend the last few minutes summarizing what agreements you have reached so far as opposed to just continuing to talk about various issues until the time expires. Practice saying something like the following:

> *"I see we are running out of time today but let's take a minute to summarize where we are so we can pick up here when we meet again."*

Judges will appreciate that you were cognizant of the time and provided a summary of where both parties were leaving the negotiation.

Quiz Yourself

1. **True or False:** A good agenda benefits not just the negotiators but the judges as well.

2. **In setting an agenda, it is important to …**
   a. Thank your opponent for agreeing to use one.
   b. Follow the agenda throughout the negotiation.
   c. Get the wording of the agenda exactly as you want it (even if it means having two separate agendas).
   d. Do none of the above.

3. **True or False.** You should wait until after the information gathering phase to set your agenda because you should use the information obtained to help identify the issues that need to be discussed.

4. **True or False.** It is effective to link issues together because your movement on issue can work as leverage to get movement from the opposing side on another issue.

5. **Which of the following statements is not true?**
   a. A summary at the end of the negotiation is necessary only if you reach an agreement.
   b. You should summarize at the end of the entire negotiation.
   c. Summarizing allows everyone to stay on the same page.
   d. You should summarize as the negotiation progresses.

Chapter 6

 # Using the Whiteboard Effectively

There is nothing more amusing than the start of a negotiation between two adversarial teams. You can usually tell in the first five minutes of the negotiation how the rest of the round will work out. Tensions run high and everyone is so anxious. Slowly things settle down as both teams get through their well-rehearsed introductions and, just as the parties get to the agenda, the action starts. That's right folks—it's time for Battle of the Boards! One person heads for the marker. The other side heads for the marker. One side writes their agenda on the board. The other side takes the marker and adjusts the agenda. Next thing you know everyone is focused on the board and no one is talking at the table. Oh brother.

Avoid the battle of the boards! The whiteboard can be a useful tool, but only when used appropriately. Below are some tips on when to use the board and how to use it effectively when you do use it.

Use the Board Only When Necessary

There is no requirement that you use the board in every round. Use of the board can actually be a distraction, and we have seen rounds where the board hurt more than helped the organization of the negotiation. If the negotiation facts provide several numbers or include numerous complicated issues, you should use the board to help you stay organized. If your opponent jumps up to use the board, you should also probably show the judges you are capable of using the board too (we wouldn't want the judges thinking those that wrote on the board were the ones in control of the negotiation). However, if your negotiation is simple and there is really nothing to write on the board, avoid using the board just for the sake of using the board. Teams that unnecessarily use the board typically get comments from the judges that the board was a waste of time.

If you do decide to use the board, knowing why you are using it is important. The purpose of the board is to keep the negotiation organized and to allow the judges to follow along with what the teams are doing. The purpose is not to cause a fight with the other team. The purpose is not to one-up the other side by showing you got to the board first. It simply does not matter who writes on the board first. A good team will effectively use the board to move the negotiation along and keep the negotiation organized even if their opponent was the first one to touch the marker.

As you are preparing for your negotiation, think about whether the facts are complex enough or whether there are enough issues that use of the board would be helpful to keep track of terms. If so, use the board for that purpose.

Give Yourself Space to Write

We couldn't begin to count the number of negotiation rounds we have seen where teams write their agenda up on the right side of the board, only to run out of room and succumb to drawing arrows randomly all over the board to keep track of terms. When you write on the board, keep in mind that the parties and judges have to be able to see the writing, but anticipate that there will be multiple offers to keep track of and several options to discuss. You want to avoid getting half way through the round and running out of room due to poor planning. There is no need to draw arrows or erase. Give yourself plenty of room from the beginning by starting on the left side of the board.

Use a Black Marker

Prior to leaving for competition, make sure you have black markers with you. Although most competitions will have markers in the classroom, you never know exactly what will be provided. You could be provided with only red markers. If you use a red marker, you will notice the judges and opposing team squinting from across the room trying to figure out what you wrote.

Always write on the board with black markers because black markers are the easiest to read from a distance. Red, green, and even blue tend to fade due to the glare from classroom lighting, and judges will struggle to read anything written in those colors. If your judges are sitting relatively close, there is less of a concern. However, you will have enough problems to deal with at competition. Get rid of this risk before you even get on the plane.

Write Legibly

Good penmanship is required anytime you use the whiteboard. Practice using the board as you prepare for competition. The person with the best handwriting should be the team member at the board. Some people feel very uncomfortable standing up and writing on the spot in front of other people. It can be nerve wracking. You are constantly thinking, "Did I forget something? Did I spell that right? How should I word that?" You might even deliberately write messy just in case you spelled something wrong with the hope others won't notice. Bad idea. Find a better solution. Only write words you know how to spell. Plan out how you are going to phrase things. Practice so you don't forget terms. Do whatever it takes because if you decide to step up to the board, you have to write legibly and you have to write big enough that people can read the words from a distance.

A few more tips. First, print all your letters rather than writing in cursive because printing is simply easier to read. Second, always use phrases rather than full sentences. No one wants to wait while someone is writing complete sentences on the board. Everyone is there to negotiate and the board should add to the negotiation rather than distract from it.

Don't Erase Your Opponent's Information

During a round, you may have a desire to erase information that the other side has written on the board. Maybe you are out of space. Maybe the board is starting to look confusing. Maybe you just don't like the other team's offer. It sounds harmless if you are erasing for a good reason, but it is rude. It will offend the judges and it will likely offend your opponent.

Avoid erasing information. In fact, it can be effective to leave old information on the board and add new terms next to the old information because it shows to all how flexible you have been with the other side. The judges can visually see where you started and the movement of both parties. If a term needs to be erased for clarity, be sure to communicate to the other side before just erasing the information. Asking your opponent if it is okay to erase their information will avoid the appearance that you are arrogant or rude.

Don't Become a Secretary

Imagine this. You are up at the board writing your agenda and the opposing side asks you to write up another term for them. No problem. Now assume the other side asks you to write up an offer for them. Then another offer. Then another offer. At this point, you no longer look like a lawyer, you look like a secretary for your opponent. Some teams actually implement this as part of their strategy. They will try to make it look like they are giving orders to the person at the board and thus in control of the negotiation.

Don't let this happen to you. If the other side asks you to add a term to the agenda—definitely add the term. If the other team starts to make you their secretary, however, stand your ground.

Hand your marker to the other side and let them come up to the board themselves. Write what you want on the board and then sit back down at the table.

If they continue to insist you do all the writing, use their persistence to your advantage. Tell them you are willing to write their terms on the board if it will help the negotiation progress. Tell them you are there to get a deal for your client and if writing their terms on the board helps get the deal done, you are happy to assist them. At this point, you will have shown your resistance to becoming a secretary and will rather look like a cooperative negotiator being flexible to get the deal done.

Don't Get Lost While Your Partner Is at the Board

Let's talk about the person who is not at the board. What should you do while your partner is away from the table? Sit silently and watch your partner write? Certainly not. The other side will already be doing that and the negotiation will quickly turn into a very awkward silence as everyone in the room just sits and watches one person write on the board.

If you are the one sitting at the table you have a very important job. You have to keep talking. You should be making eye contact with the other side and should continue to negotiate or explain the ideas being written on the board. You can provide a justification for a term your partner is writing on the board. You can state the agenda while your partner writes the agenda on the board. You can add further details about what your partner is writing. The important thing is that you continue to move the negotiation along as your partner writes.

Your partner should be talking as well. That's right! Talking and writing at the same time! Even as you are thinking about whether you spelled a word right or whether you are forgetting something, you have to contribute to the conversation. There are high expectations if you want first place. The room looks off balance if three people are at the table and one is just alone quietly writing on the whiteboard. In fact, from our experience, it looks crazy. It is a negotiation with three people while poor lonely-board-guy writes away. Try to have everyone continue the negotiation even if the board becomes a part of it.

Practice this over and over. It is hard, but your ability to make your trip to the white board look natural and more conversational is key to your success.

Avoid Overusing the Board

By this time, we know what you are thinking: "I had no idea all of this went into using a whiteboard. I thought I could just run up there and jot some stuff down and take a seat." Good thing you are reading this book! Hang in there because we have one more thing to add.

Our last tip on the board: use the board sparingly. If you put something on the board, you should refer back to it and you should use what you have on the board to help facilitate the negotiation. However, you must refrain from becoming a frog jumping up and down from table to board over and over again. You start to look silly. Let us paint the picture for you:

You make an offer. Your partner jumps up to the board to write it down. Your partner sits down. The opposing team makes a counter-offer. Your partner gets back up to the board to write it down. You make another offer. Up goes your partner again. And again. And again. It gets even funnier when your partner starts walking toward the board, but the other side starts to talk, forcing your partner to stand and wait. Sometimes they wait for quite a long time. Just standing there—looking silly. Eventually, your partner sits down, just to get up again a few minutes later.

At this point the judges are quite entertained by all the jumping up and down. Unfortunately, they are entertained by your partner's frog like movements and not by their negotiation skills.

Use the board. Write up offers. But be aware of how often you are jumping up and down. Every negotiation is different, but you may need to be patient and just write the final agreement for each issue as it is reached. You may not be able to write every offer made by each team.

Quiz Yourself

1. **True or False:** You should always find a way to use the whiteboard during a negotiation round.

2. **What is the purpose of the white board?**
   a. To keep the negotiation organized.
   b. To help the judges follow the negotiation.
   c. To intimidate your opponent.
   d. a and b.

3. **What should be your first choice in color of marker for the board?**

4. **True or False.** If you run out of space to write on the board, you should erase the information your opponent has written.

5. **When your partner is writing on the board, you should:**
   a. Watch quietly.
   b. Instruct your partner what to write, line by line.
   c. Stay involved in the negotiation by talking with your partner and to the opposing side.
   d. None of the above.

Chapter 7

Using the Law Effectively

If you have never participated in a negotiation competition, you might be thinking, "Negotiation is not that hard. All I have to do is talk!" Nothing could be further from the truth. To be an effective negotiator, you have to know and understand the law, and you have to use it effectively in the negotiation.

The Type of Law You Will Encounter

For the most part, the law you will encounter in a negotiation competition will involve a statute. Occasionally, relevant case law is attached or referenced in the problem; however, asking students to know all the case law in a particular jurisdiction is a rarity for a negotiation competition. Usually if there is a reference to a case, the relevant language from the case is included or the case name is given. Typically the law given will include one statute or a series of statutes.

Creating Arguments Based on the Law

If there is law referenced in the negotiation problem, your job is to make it favor your side. As you read through the law, look for ways the law can favor both sides. Most problems are set up so each side can create strong arguments under the law. Perhaps there are some statutes in favor of the plaintiff and other statutes in favor of the defendant. Perhaps the statute contains vague or ambiguous words that can be interpreted in different ways. Always look for "buzz words" that can be used by either party. For example, the words "reasonable," "fair," "clear," or similar terms can always be interpreted differently by each side. If the law appears to favor one side more than the other, look deeper. There is always an argument for your client.

Let's take an example. Assume the following statute is provided:

> § 22: A written document designating a surrogate to make health care decisions for a principal is a valid living will if it is in writing, made in the presence of two subscribing adult witnesses, and clearly sets forth an intent by the principal to designate another to make medical decisions regarding the principal's care.

Do you notice any language that could require subjective judgment and could lead to creating arguments for either side? Hopefully the "clearly sets forth an intent ... to make medical decisions" is screaming out to you. Each side potentially has an argument that the document demonstrated or failed to demonstrate a clear intent.

This law is actually based on the same ABA Negotiation Problem referenced in Chapter 4, where Judy went into surgery for a nose job. Prior to the surgery, Judy filled out the standard medical emergency form which stated, *"In the event of emergency, or if a medical decision is needed and I am unable to consent, then I direct that you contact:* Josh Thompson, who is my fiancé, at 504-222-2121." The surgery did not go as planned and Judy ended up in a coma. Josh, the fiancé, wanted to keep Judy on life support and Judy's parents, the opposing party, wanted to discontinue life support. The question became whether the emergency form was a valid living will. If so, Josh would get to make the decisions. If not, the parents could terminate life support.

The facts stated that the document was properly signed and witnessed. The only issue was whether Judy intended to have Josh make medical decisions on her behalf. Our students represented the parents and were sure they had a losing case under the law. They came into practice and told us the document is a living will because it clearly designates Josh to make the medical decisions. They failed to realize that the law is rarely clear.

After further thought, the students agreed that the parents had great arguments under the law. First, the statute requires the document show a clear intent that the person should make the medical decisions. The emergency form signed by Judy, however, only said to "contact" Josh. It did not say that Josh should be the person to make the medical decision. Perhaps he should be contacted because he was a local friend who knew how to get in touch with Judy's parents if something happened. Furthermore, designating someone as an emergency contact does not carry the type of clear intent necessary to make someone a surrogate. Typically, surrogacy documents are thought about and drafted in advance with the help of an attorney. An emergency contact form signed immediately before plastic surgery does not have the requisite intent that the person was trying to make someone a surrogate.

Remember, there is always an argument that can be made for your client. You need to think of your strongest arguments and think of your opponent's strongest arguments so you can refute them if they are brought up in the negotiation. If you can't find them, dig deeper.

Using the Law Effectively in the Round

Okay, you have thought of all your arguments and opponents' arguments. Now what do you do with them? When should you bring the law into the negotiation? How do you effectively use the legal arguments in the negotiation?

A. When Should You Bring the Law into the Negotiation?

The answer is easy. Always. Using the law gives your side power in the negotiation. If you are comfortable talking about the law, your opponent will be more concerned about the results at trial. Your opponent is likely to give in to what you want now if your opponent is scared about what will happen later.

When we say always bring the law in, we do not mean bring the law in throughout the entire negotiation. Rather, think carefully about at what point during the negotiation the law will be most effective. Sometimes it will be appropriate to allude to the strengths of the law in your introduction. If you have strong arguments that your client would prevail at trial, an introduction might start off with that notion. You may let the opposing side know immediately that you feel strongly your client would prevail, but you are willing to work with the other side to try to find resolution. For example, if you represent the parents in the above negotiation with Josh, your introduction might include the following idea:

"It is unfortunate to have to be at the table discussing Judy's life. However, Jim and Susan Kerr are confident Judy did not intend for the emergency form to name Josh as a medical surrogate. Thus, without a valid living will, Jim and Susan have authority to make decisions about their daughter's medical care. Jim and Susan do care about Josh, however, and we are here in hopes we can work something out with Josh so that both parties can be comfortable with the decision."

You can also bring up more specific arguments about the law as they become relevant during the negotiation. For example, at the point the opposing side argues that Josh was appointed surrogate, you would bring up the specific argument about the language stating Josh should be "contacted," rather than stating Josh had the right to make a medical decision.

If the opposing side does not bring up the law, you can still introduce it later in the negotiation to get movement from the other side. There will be times when the other side simply won't budge from their offers and the table is at a standstill. This is a great time to remind your opponent of why settlement is to their benefit. Use the law to demonstrate what could happen if your opponent does not move.

B. How Do You Effectively Use the Law Once You Introduce It?

Two key points you should remember. First, you will never get your opponent to admit that your arguments under the law are correct. Do not have high hopes that your opponent will hear your argument and say "You know, I think you are right. We are likely to lose if this case goes to trial." It won't happen. But that is okay. Your goal in bringing in the law is not to receive that type of response from the other side. Your goal is to let the other side know you are not scared of the law and that you are a competent attorney. Making your argument one time establishes this point. Do not continue to argue back and forth about the law for the entire negotiation. Make your point one time and move on.

Second, always transition immediately from your legal argument to a proposal. Stating your legal argument and leaving the table silent is ineffective. Only one result will occur: the other side will make a counter-argument. This gets the parties nowhere. Instead, make your point about the law and then move the negotiation forward by linking your argument to your next offer. Under this approach, you are able to show your strength but continue to work toward a deal.

Remember, if the opposing side brings up the law and you fail to respond, you will appear weak to the judges and to the opposing side. Be prepared to discuss your arguments about the law and don't shy away from your opportunity to do so.

Quiz Yourself

1. **True or False.** Good negotiators avoid bringing law into a negotiation so they can focus on the issues at hand.

2. **True or False.** You should focus on your opponent's arguments under the law as well as your own.

3. **What are some "buzz words" found in negotiation problems that might help you create arguments and counter-arguments?**

4. **True or False.** Before moving on to a new issue, make sure your opponent understands and agrees with your interpretation of the law.

5. **True or False.** You should use the law as a way to threaten litigation during the negotiation.

Chapter 8

 ## Techniques to Getting a Good Deal

Okay, so you made it past the handshake. You asked information gathering questions. You set your agenda. You have your legal arguments ready to go. Finally, the reason why you came to the table: the deal. How can you get the best deal possible for your client? Below are our tips.

Put Your Client's Interests Before Your Own

A common problem for most negotiators: your ego. Too often a negotiator's ego precludes the negotiator from reaching a good deal. Your ego can interfere in a variety of ways. Below are two examples.

A. "I Am Determined to Get More"

You want to be the best. You are used to being the best. Thus, you naturally want to get the BEST deal. Sounds great on the surface. Who doesn't want the best deal? The problem occurs when you allow your desire to get the best deal overtake your client's interests. If the opposing side is offering you a deal that is attractive to your client, push for more. Test the waters. See what you can get. However, you must know when to stop pushing and recognize that even though you would like to get more, the deal being offered is within your client's limits and your client would want you to take it. Don't let your own desire to look good and get a great deal interfere with getting a deal that looks good to your client.

B. "That Guy Is a Jerk"

Another way your ego can interfere with getting a good deal: the opposing side irritates you. Perhaps opposing counsel are rude. They interrupt you. They mock you. They play silly negotiating games that annoy you. Your natural reaction will be to make sure you return the favor. You will want to be sure their tactics and behavior do not pay off. As a result, you will be hesitant to give in. Be careful and take note of why you are not conceding to their offers. Is it because you have too much pride and conceding will make you look like they won? If so, that is not a good reason to stand firm. If you are letting your own pride get in the way of reaching agreement, you are not serving your client. You are serving yourself. Don't let your own pride get in the way of bringing home a good deal for your client.

Whenever you are negotiating on behalf of your client, your main objective is to look out for your client's interests. If your client needs a deal, don't let your own interests and desires get in the way. After all, you can't get a great deal if you never get a deal at all. Don't let your desire to get more prevent you from reaching an agreement. Don't let the opposing side's behavior affect your ability to negotiate and look out for your client's interests. Get the best deal possible, but get a deal your client would be happy with (even if you would not be).

Actively Listen

People love to hear themselves talk. In fact, most people will be more than happy to continue talking as long as they have someone willing to listen. Use this to your advantage. When people speak, information is revealed. Listen carefully for that information because it will help you understand the other side's underlying interests and can help you find the weaknesses in your opponent's case. Information can also help you determine just how far the other side is willing to go to get a deal.

Listening actively is not as easy as it sounds. It is a skill that must be developed over time with practice. When we say "listen actively," you must do more than just hear the words that are being said. You must also hear the underlying meaning or message those words are conveying. Let's take a few examples.

First, assume you are negotiating an employment opportunity for your client. During the negotiation, opposing counsel mentions the collegial working environment at the office. He explains that the employees at the office spend a lot of time together. They not only have lunch together, but often have dinner together as well. They even see each other on the weekends. If you merely listen to the opposing counsel's words, you might think your client is about to join an office with a fun, cooperative working environment. If you listen actively, however, you might start to wonder why the employees are having dinner together. Is it because they are returning to work after dinner and not going home? Why are they seeing each other so often on the weekends? Is it because they are in the office working? Maybe the underlying message is that the employees are spending so much time together because they work long hours.

Let's take another example. Assume your client is suing a mechanic claiming the mechanic installed faulty brakes in your client's vehicle. Your client was involved in an accident as a result of the poor brake job and is seeking $30,000 for the cost of his injuries and for his pain and suffering. Assume at some point during the negotiation, opposing counsel offers you $30,000 as long as your client agrees to sign a release of liability and a confidentiality agreement. If you are merely listening to the words of opposing counsel, you are likely to jump at the $30,000 figure. However, if you listen to the meaning of that offer, you may realize you should not jump at the number, but instead ask further questions regarding their request for a confidentiality agreement. Why does the mechanic want this settlement kept confidential? Has this happened before? Are there other potential lawsuits in the works? If so, you may be able to get the mechanic to give even more than $30,000.

Most negotiators are so busy thinking about what they want to say next or how to respond to opposing counsel's argument, that they fail to really listen to what is being said. If you are thinking of your next point, you are not listening. Slow down and listen actively.

Don't Panic Over Which Side Makes the First Offer

Students frequently worry that they should not make the first offer in a negotiation. After all, if you open with an offer asking for $10,000 and the other side was willing to give you $20,000, you have lost your chance to receive more money. Allowing your opponent to make the first offer lets you evaluate how much they may be willing to give and lets you avoid making an offer that limits your possibilities.

Being the one to start the bargaining process also has its advantages. By choosing to make the opening offer, you are able to anchor the negotiation and set the parameters of what type of offers will be acceptable. Imagine this. Your opponent was in a car accident and had high hopes that he would become rich as a result of the settlement. He comes into the negotiation thinking he might receive $40,000 to $50,000. If you start the bidding process and offer $200, his tune is likely to change quickly. You will immediately set the tone of a negotiation in the hundreds and low thousands rather than have to waste time trying to get him to back off an offer of $40,000.

Whether you should make an offer first or let your opponent do so often depends on the circumstances of the case. Think about the facts before you and decide whether it is most effective to anchor the negotiation or most effective to see what your opponent has to say.

Start as High as You Can Reasonably Justify

Many negotiators go into the negotiation with the same thought: "Those who start big get big results." Thus, those negotiators tend to make large opening offers. That strategy doesn't always work. Extreme offers have consequences.

First, if your opponent thinks your offer is unreasonable, you risk the chance your opponent either walks out of the negotiation or responds with an equally ridiculous offer. Either way, you are unlikely to reach a settlement. If your offer is extreme on one end and your opponent's offer is extreme on the other end, you are not likely to find the settlement zone between the two.

Let us provide a true story that illustrates this point nicely. A bank loaned a business man $1 million to start a new business. The business failed. The businessman failed to pay back the loan and the bank sued the businessman to recover the $1 million plus interest. In the first (and only) negotiation between the bank and the businessman, the businessman's lawyer made the first offer. He asked the bank's lawyer, "How much is the bank going to pay my client to make this go away?" The bank's lawyer walked out of the negotiation and the bank instructed its lawyer not to enter into any further negotiations with the businessman. The businessman's lawyer later tried to be reasonable and reopen negotiations. The bank refused to negotiate. The case went to trial and the bank won. The businessman had to pay back the full amount of the loan, interest, and the bank's attorney's fees. Bad move on the part of the businessman's lawyer. Had the businessman's lawyer started off with a more reasonable offer, the businessman would have likely been able to significantly reduce the debt owed to the bank.

Big offers don't always mean big results. If the offers are too big, they often mean big loss of opportunity. On the other hand, if you don't start big you could miss potential money in the pot. So what should you do? Start as high as you can reasonably justify. If you can't make your offer sound reasonable, it is too high. However, you need to take the time to find ways to make a higher offer sound reasonable so you have the potential to have bigger results.

React to Outrageous Offers

If your opponent makes an extreme offer, you must let them know that they are well out of the ballpark. Too often we hear an offer that is far from the settlement zone, yet our students' response is "well, you are a little bit off." This reaction gives the other side the wrong impression and the opposing side will start making smaller jumps because you did not suggest the offer was unreasonable. If you hear an outrageous offer, you need to let them know just how outrageous it is. You need to react.

First, your non-verbal expression and body language should show your shock at their offer. Don't act calm and show no expression in your face. You need to look surprised. Perhaps your eyes get big. Maybe your jaw falls open. Maybe your body shifts back in your chair. Just do something. Don't simply proceed as if the number was reasonable.

Second, you should verbally let the other side know how far off they are. Tell the other side that the offer is far outside an acceptable range and tell them they are going to need to come up with a more reasonable offer to get the negotiation started. They are unlikely to accommodate your request because they don't want to "double-bid." If your opponent won't come up with another offer, make sure your counter-offer is just as ridiculous as their first offer. If you expect the dispute to settle for around $15,000–$20,000 and your opponent came in at $100,000, your counter offer should be $1000. You want to make a statement. You want your statement to scream "You are far off!" If you make a reasonable offer, your verbal and non-verbal reactions will have little effect. If you respond to the $100,000 offer with an offer for $10,000, your opponent will continue to bid high because the technique is working. A response of $10,000 also leaves little room to move, and you will need a lot of room to get your opponent down from $100,000.

Bottom line? React! Make sure they know they need to make a big jump.

Think About the Timing and Placement of Your Justifications

An effective negotiator makes their opponent think the opponent is the one getting the good deal. After all, no one wants to walk away from a deal thinking "I just got worked!" Your opponent wants to walk away proud, saying, "I just got a great deal for my client!" If you can make them feel this way, they are more likely to accept your offers. Thus, it is your job to convince your opponent that your offers are favorable for their client (or at least fair). How do you do this? Justify. Explain why your offers are reasonable and why they serve your opponent's interests.

Justifications for your offers often come straight from the information provided in the negotiation problem. You can use the law to explain why your offer is reasonable. After all, if you have strong arguments under the law, the deal will sound favorable to your opponent because it will be better than losing at trial. You can also use facts from the problem to explain why your offer is reasonable. Assume you are representing a player entering the National Basketball Association. You sit down to negotiate an endorsement deal with Gatorade and ask for $3 million per year. Your offer will appear reasonable if you are able to explain that your client led his team to the finals in NCAA Basketball tournament by averaging thirty points a game and making ten blocks during the tournament. Convince Gatorade that his fame linked to their product will bring more sales to Gatorade in the long term than a mere $3 million. You want Gatorade's attorneys walking away saying "I can't believe I got that player for only $3 million. What a deal!"

A. Think Carefully About When You Make Your Justifications

If you justify at the wrong time, your justifications may actually make your offer appear unreasonable. A justification made too early gives the impression your offer is weak and thus needs justification. Imagine this. You sit down with Gatorade's attorneys and say something like the following: "Our client is looking to make $3 million. This is reasonable because our client led his team to the finals in the NCAA basketball tournament. He averaged 30 points a game. He made 10 blocks. He is worth that amount." Making the justifications at the moment you mention your first offer may actually make your adversary think the $3 million number is high because you were so desperate to explain why it was fair.

It often is more effective to hold off on your justification until you hear your opponent's response. Put your number on the table and see how the opposing side reacts before giving your justifications. The conversation might go something like this:

> You: "Our client is looking to make $3 million/year for the term of the endorsement."
> Gatorade's attorney: "3 million? Your client is no Tim Duncan!"
> You: "He may not be Tim Duncan yet, but he is certainly on that road. His statistics just in this last NCAA tournament demonstrate his potential for success. In the most recent NCAA tournament, he led his team to the championship. He had the highest point average out of all players in the tournament and dominated defensively with ten blocked shots. Don't you want to be the company he is associated with as he becomes the new Tim Duncan?"

By holding off on your justification when you originally make an offer, you appear confident in your number and suggest the offer needs no justification. Rather, you assume its reasonableness is apparent. You can later justify the offer if its reasonableness is questioned by the opposing side.

B. Save Some Justifications for Future Offers

Perhaps you have multiple reasons why your offer is reasonable. Not only did your client perform well in his past season, but he has an endorsement offer from PowerAde for $2 million per year he is also considering. Don't bring up all of your justifications at one time. Save some justifications for subsequent offers. Start with the justification that your client performed well last season and save the PowerAde deal as an incentive to get Gatorade to move up as the negotiation progresses. For example, if Gatorade ultimately makes an offer of $1.8 million/year in the negotiation, you can tell them "PowerAde has offered him more than that and you are a much bigger company with potential to make even more from endorsements by my client."

C. Don't Overjustify

Less is more. Just as a justification at the wrong time can make your offer less convincing, too much justification can make your offer less convincing. If you are trying too hard to make your offer look reasonable, it can appear that you are overcompensating because the offer is really weak. The strongest justifications are short and concise. Just state your reason and let the other side respond. Don't feel a need to overexplain.

Furthermore, justifying every offer that hits the table or spending too much time on your justification for one offer can hold up the negotiation. Remember you have to keep the numbers moving and you should not feel obligated to justify every offer put on the table. Start with strong justifications, but as the bargaining progresses remember it is okay just to haggle (i.e., go back and forth with the numbers without justifications).

Don't Negotiate Against Yourself

The ultimate faux pas in a negotiation: the double-bid. Imagine you represent a construction company and you are looking to hire a concrete supplier. You offer to pay the concrete supplier $20 per yard of concrete. The concrete supplier says that $20 is too low. You offer $25. He says your offer is still too low. You offer $30. You are raising your offer without getting any bids from the supplier. If you continue, the supplier will keep going until you end up at your bottom line. By continuing to raise your offer, you are negotiating against yourself.

Effective negotiators avoid negotiating against themselves. Rather, before making a new offer, make sure you get a counter-offer from the other side. By getting a counter-offer, you nail down a number the other side is willing to work with and can move the numbers from there. You are much more likely to get a good deal for your client if you get them to pick a number and get them to move down from that number as you move up.

Thus, if you make an offer and your opponent says your offer is too low, instead of raising your offer, ask your opponent what price your opponent was looking for. Get your adversary to put a number on the table before ever offering another number.

Look for Creative Solutions That Meet Both Parties' Interests

Often deals are lost because the attorneys focus on the opposing side's position and fail to listen for the opposing side's underlying interests. A position is what one client wants. An interest is why the client wants it.

Imagine this. You represent a father seeking custody of his daughter. His position is that he wants custody of his daughter on Mondays, Wednesdays, and Saturdays. His ex-wife wants custody every other week for the full week. If you focus only on the couple's positions, you will never reach an agreement. If you discover the couple's interests — why each person wants that particular custody arrangement — you may be able to find creative ways to make both parties happy. Perhaps the father wants custody on Mondays, Wednesdays, and Saturdays because he wants his daughter to play soccer and those are the practice/game days. Perhaps the mother wants custody every other week because she has an out-of-town boyfriend and she wants to be able to visit him. If you discover these underlying interests, you can be creative and award custody every other week as long as the ex-wife agrees to take the daughter to soccer every Monday, Wednesday, and Saturday.

Consider another example. Joe and Phil are brothers. Their father passed away and his will devised Joe all of his property. However, the father's other son, Phil, was born after the will was executed. Under state law, a child born after execution of the will is entitled to recover an equal proportion of the devisor's assets if the child can show the devisor would have intended the unborn child to receive part of the assets. The brothers end up in a dispute over the property. Joe wants the property because it has sentimental value and he worries if Phil has any interest in the property he will force a sale of the house. Phil wants the property because he has information that the land underneath the home has valuable minerals in it and he will be rich if he can get a 50% interest in the land. If Joe and Phil's lawyers focus only on the law and what each brother is entitled to, they are unlikely to reach settlement. Joe will not give Phil an interest in the property because his father left it to him and he cannot risk Phil selling it. Phil will only be satisfied if he gets an interest in the property because he knows his father would have intended him to share in his estate. If the parties' focus is on why Phil is or is not entitled to a 50% interest in the land, they are unlikely to find settlement.

If the parties focus instead on each side's underlying interests — the reasons why each side wants the land — a settlement is within reach. If Joe discovers Phil is only interested in the land because of the minerals and Phil discovers Joe just wants to keep the home for sentimental reasons, the brothers can agree that Phil is owner of the home and Joe is owner of the mineral rights below the land.

Discovering the underlying interests of the parties allows the attorneys to come up with creative solutions to meet both parties' interests. During a negotiation, you should always be listening for the parties' underlying interests and looking for creative ways to make a deal.

Look for Opportunities to Make a Package Deal

Leveraging issues against each other is a great way to maximize your results. Rather than negotiating one term of the deal at a time, use the terms against each other to get more for your client. For example, only give up more money if your opponent is going to give you movement on another term in the negotiation. One way to effectively leverage issues is to create a package deal. Rather than making offers separately for each issue, let the opposing side know where you stand on all of the issues at one time. Then, when your opponent asks for movement in one area, you can make movement contingent on movement by them in another area.

Imagine this. You are negotiating a deal for a professional sports team to use a stadium and the following four items are at issue (i) rent for the stadium; (ii) advertising within the stadium; (iii) parking fees; and (iv) length of the term. You could individually negotiate each of these terms. First talk about the rent and try to reach a number both sides agree on. Then discuss advertising. Then parking. Then the length of the term. You will likely be able to reach agreement on each individual term. However, if you discuss all four items at the same time by creating a package deal, you will have the opportunity to reach a better deal for your client. When opposing counsel makes a counter-offer on the rent, instead of just accepting that offer you can link it to movement in advertising. So, instead of just agreeing to $20,000/month in rent, you can agree to $20,000/month in rent so long as you receive 100% of the profits for parking and get 50% of the advertising space. Package deals are a great tool to assist you in receiving something every time you give something up.

A package deal also saves considerable time in reaching a deal. Rather than taking time to independently discuss each issue, you simultaneously discuss several at once and the result is a much quicker deal. Just remember to stay organized. Use of the board is good idea if you are creating a package offer.

Learn to Be Comfortable with Silence

Everyone fears silence and as a result silence can be a powerful tool at the negotiation table. Imagine you make a brilliant argument about why your client deserves more compensation. So brilliant, in fact, that the other side doesn't even have a response. They have to think. The table falls silent.

What now? Usually, the silence is so uncomfortable that you feel the need to keep talking. You ruin your brilliant point by following it up with another point. Your inability to deal with silence just let the other side off the hook. By making an additional point or by moving the negotiation along, your opponent no longer has to respond to your argument. If you had let the table remain silent you would have forced them to respond and they would have likely responded with a better offer. Don't fear silence. Often it will cause great results.

Silence also works well as a response to an opposing offer. Sometimes the best response to your opponent's offer will be to say nothing. Just let the awkwardness of the silence take hold of the table and you might get them to double-, or even triple-bid. Silence makes people do things they would not otherwise do. Avoid letting it change your behavior, but feel free to let the other side try to fill the space. They are likely to do so with information or offers that will be beneficial to your client.

Quiz Yourself

1. **True or False.** Listening is common sense and most people are natural listeners.

2. **True or False.** The negotiation is not won or lost by making the first offer.

3. **How high should your first offer be?**
   a. $20,000 above your bottom line.
   b. $20,000 above your ideal agreement.
   c. High enough to shock the opposing side.
   d. As high as you can reasonably justify.

4. **If your opponent makes an outrageous offer, you should:**

   a. React and make sure they know they need to make a big jump.

   b. Proceed as if the numbers are reasonable.

   c. Act calm and show no expression on your face.

   d. Look to the judges and say "Do you believe this crazy offer?"

5. **How do you convince your opponent that your offers are reasonable?**

   a. Justify your offers.

   b. Explain how your offers serve your opponent's interests.

   c. Both a and b.

   d. Neither a or b.

Chapter 9

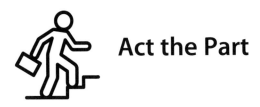

Act the Part

You have a fake client. You have a fake problem. You are in a fake conference room. Your job is to make the negotiation seem real. You must get your judges to forget the round is part of a competition and think they are watching real attorneys with a real problem. To make things harder, you have to accomplish this in an interesting and entertaining way. Even though you must appear to be a real attorney, you have no leeway to be boring and stiff. You must be interesting. You must be memorable.

Stay in Character

Stay in character from the moment you sit down at the table until the moment you walk out the door. You can't take a time out. You can't start over. You can't ask the judges questions in the middle of the round. Imagine your client is real and spoke to you about the facts before you walked into the room. Imagine your opponent is opposing counsel who has driven from miles away to meet with you to discuss the case.

Make your client seem present at the table. Speak about your client during the negotiation as if he or she really exists. If the other side makes an offer you do not like, tell them how hard it will be to sell it to your client and why. If the opposing side makes a statement which conflicts with one of the facts in your problem, do not say "That is not in our facts." Instead say, "I haven't spoken about that with my client yet" or "my client has provided me with different information."

Don't take reality overboard. Do not tell the other side you are going to step outside and call your client (and then return as if you spoke to your client outside the room). Instead, tell them you need to take a break to discuss the offers with your partner. Do not tell the other side you have a plane to catch. Instead, tell them you have limited time. You want the negotiation to seem real, but you don't want to appear fake. It is a fine balance, but an important balance.

Keep the Rounds Interesting

Your judges will typically be watching two fifty minute rounds of negotiation. The negotiations will be on the exact same problem with the exact same facts. This can be a long, painful experience. In fact, we have seen one judge actually fall asleep during the round. You need to keep the judges awake and involved in the negotiation. You need to be interesting. You need to be memorable.

There are a variety of ways to keep a negotiation interesting. Here are some tips.

A. Pay Attention to the Inflection in Your Voice

Monotone speakers tend to bore the judges. Don't have one consistent tone throughout the entire negotiation. Use your voice to react to offers, make movement, and show excitement. For example, your voice should sound excited if you are describing your client's business plan, but should sound firm if you are describing your arguments under the law. Similarly, you should not have the same tone of voice in reacting to an outrageous offer as you would if you were reacting to a reasonable offer. Let your voice show your disappointment and excitement throughout the round.

Be careful to pay attention to the volume and speed of your voice as well. Remember you have an audience other than the opposing team. You need to speak loudly enough that all the judges will hear you. Even the old ones. You need to speak slowly enough that all the judges will understand you.

B. Be Aware of Your Body Language

How you sit at a table can make a negotiation more interesting. If you slouch in your chair with your head down, you will not capture the attention of the judges. Sit up straight in your chair and make eye contact with the opposing side. Don't rock back and forth in your chair. Don't roll back and forth in your chair. Don't tap your pencil on the table. And please don't put the arm of your glasses in your mouth.

Use your body as well as your voice to react and show enthusiasm during the round. Lean in to show you are really listening and interested in what the other side is saying. Lean back if you are surprised by an outrageous offer. Use your hands as you describe your proposal. Raise an eyebrow here and there. Your facial expressions alone can make you memorable.

C. Use Humor (or at least feel comfortable laughing when the opposing side is funny)

Humor has two advantages. Not only will you get the judges to like you, but you will get your opponent to like you. People tend to give in more quickly if they like who they are giving in to. If you are relaxed and funny, or at least relaxed enough to recognize humor and laugh with the other side, the round will have a cooperative tone and you are more likely to get a deal. You are also more likely to be remembered by the judges when they are tallying their scores.

Keep in mind that the humor must be appropriate. Crude or offensive humor never belongs in the round. Never make a joke at the expense of someone else in the room. Never make a joke that could offend one of the judges watching your round. Canned humor also tends to fail. Make sure your humor is natural and spontaneous.

D. Use Real Life Examples

If you can relate an idea in your negotiation problem to a real world example, it makes your argument stronger and makes the negotiation more interesting. By using an everyday example, the other side can understand your argument at a higher level because it is similar to something they are familiar with. It also makes the negotiation come to life for the judges.

Let's take an example. Assume your client wants to open a sewing boutique that specializes in exceptional customer service. One approach in describing your client's concept to opposing counsel might be:

"The sales clerks at the boutique will have specialized training in serving customers and will have specialized training in the kinds of fabrics sold in the store. They will learn about sewing techniques customers may ask about."

Although your explanation may be accurate and clear, it is boring. Instead, it is your job to make the idea more interesting by comparing it to a similar concept everyone in the room might be familiar with:

"Our clients want to open a sewing boutique with a business model similar to Apple. If you have ever walked into an Apple store to buy a new iPhone or iPad, you notice immediately that the Apple employees are a cohesive unit. They are not your typical sales clerks. They are really technicians. They are experts in all Apple merchandise and they are eager to help the customers and explain just how amazing Apple products are and how they work. Our client's plan is similar, but the employees will know all brands of fabrics and the pros and cons of using one fabric over another. Every employee will be able to explain the most effective approach to making a variety of different sewing projects …"

By using an everyday example, you have more validity to your proposal because it has been done before and you have created a more interesting round for all involved.

E. Paint a Picture When Discussing Your Facts

Not only should you bring in real life examples, but you should make the explanation of the ideas in your problem as vivid as possible. Imagine you are asked to pitch an idea for a new restaurant to an investor. Your client's vision is to open a pizza restaurant that sells pizzas with toppings you would typically find in a Chinese restaurant. Describe the idea to opposing counsel in an exciting, vivid manner. Really paint a picture of what your client envisions.

The following does not paint a vivid picture: "Our client has an idea we are hoping your client will be interested in. He wants to open a pizza restaurant with an Asian theme. All the pizzas will have Asian toppings and the restaurant theme will combine the traditional Italian food idea with the culture of the Asian community ..."

Compare the following: "Our client has a brilliant idea that is going to be the next Benihana! Imagine this. America's most popular dish — pizza — combined with the elegance and unique taste of Asian cuisine. Your party sits down on the floor around low tables and can select from hundreds of topping combinations. One pizza might be orange chicken and cashew chicken. Another might be a beef and broccoli pizza. Can you imagine how good a fried rice pizza might taste? People will line up around the building for this. It will be an incomparable dining experience."

Whether you actually think fried rice pizza would be good, the person that sells the client's vision the best is the one who the judges will remember and the one who will walk home with the trophy. Be vivid. Be exciting. Paint a picture whenever you can.

———————

Quiz Yourself

1. Which of the following are permissible during the negotiation round?

   a. Take a time out during the round and ask the judges questions.

   b. Start over (if the other side agrees).

   c. Ask your coach for advice.

   d. None of the above.

2. **True or False:** If your opponent makes a statement that conflicts with the facts you were provided, you should tell them the facts you were given are different.

3. Which of the following are ways you can keep the round interesting for the judges.

   a. Use humor.

   b. Be aware of your body language and voice inflection.

   c. Use real life examples.

   d. All of the above.

4. **True or False.** When providing examples during a negotiation, you should use vivid details to make your example come to life.

5. **True or False.** You can exaggerate the truth of the facts if the purpose is to make your client's story more interesting.

Chapter 10

 ## Tactics to Look Out For

To win a negotiation competition, you must think of negotiation as a sport. You need to have a plan for success. In fact, you and your partner should spend weeks working on your strategy. Your worthy opponents will likely do the same. Let's take a minute and discuss some of the tactics you could encounter from your opponent during competition and even in real life negotiations. Note: these are not tactics we recommend. These are tactics we want you to be aware of in case they happen to you.

Over the years, some teams have started to resort to gimmicks. Gimmicks spread quickly. Before you know it, the gimmicks become typical clichéd strategic moves by your opponent. You must be able to adjust to any gimmick or negotiation approach you encounter. Be on the lookout for the following three tactics we have seen on a regular basis.

Anger and Constant Interruptions

The first time we witnessed the "yelling/interruption" approach was in the final round of a regional competition. Our students went up against an extremely aggressive team and struggled to maintain composure. They started off with their introductions but could not get past the first sentence before the opposing team interrupted them. They were patient at first, but the opposing team continued to speak over them. The result was our team failed to get a single idea on the table. In addition, the opposing team raised their voices in anger when our students refused to accept the first offer presented. The opposing team stood up and yelled at our students, asking our students why they would not take the deal.

Needless to say, our team did not fare well when it came time for the ranking process. We were ranked low because we were unable to control the negotiation. The entire round was spent with the other side pushing their first offer and yelling at us when we didn't take it. The round was not effective for either team.

Big secret: the yelling approach only works in the movies. In real life, no one thinks being disrespectful to opposing counsel is effective. Unfortunately, teams often confuse being a competitive negotiator with being a jerk. The two are not the same and it can be incredibly frustrating to compete against a team that is so aggressive they don't listen or allow you to speak. You must do something to stop them or you will lose the round.

If you find yourself in a round where your opponent continuously interrupts or talks over you, don't tolerate it. You must call them out on their behavior. Find an opportunity to communicate to them that the negotiation cannot continue without both sides being able to speak. Try to set some ground rules for the negotiation and stress the importance of both sides being able to speak in order for the negotiation to continue. If the other side does not agree or agrees but fails to follow through, tell them both teams need to take a break to think about how the negotiation can proceed.

Ultimately, if a team will not allow you to speak and will not engage in the process, you should walk out. Give a warning first. Walking out is a last resort and you should be sure there is no other way to get the negotiation to progress. However, there may be a time when you need to walk out of the room and end the negotiation (even in competition). That was the advice of our judges in the round above. They told our students the biggest mistake they made was not walking away.

So, when you are faced with someone who has difficulty communicating: (1) set ground rules and explain that you are not willing to negotiate under the current circumstances; (2) if the behavior continues, explain that you will need to end the negotiation if the behavior remains the same; and (3) hold firm on the promise and walk out if necessary.

No Offers, Combined with Prolonged Information Gathering

The first time we witnessed the "no offer" approach, it was painful to watch. One team was making offers and providing justifications while the other team kept asking questions. Each time the offering team tried to make an offer or ask the opposing team for a counteroffer, the opposing team would respond with more questions. The offer/question pattern went on for a solid thirty minutes (out of a fifty-minute round).

Initially, it looked like a lack of preparation by the questioning team, but it eventually became clear that the questioning was an intentional tactic. After thirty minutes of questions and no offers, the team asking all the questions decided to take a break. They took a five-minute break and came back in ready to roll. Instead of continuing to ask questions, they put a package offer on the board. The offer was targeted perfectly because if the other side failed to agree to the offer, they would run the risk of running out of time with no deal at all. So, of course, the team accepted the package and the questioning team looked like the savior of the round by coming up with the brilliant package that could make everyone happy.

The strategy is intriguing: gather information for as long as possible, then go outside and come up with the perfect deal that your opponent cannot refuse. If you don't recognize what your opponent is doing, you will likely become frustrated and will most certainly end up bidding against yourself. Your opponents will receive credit for being the team that caused the negotiation to progress.

There are different approaches to deal with an opponent who uses this strategy. Here are a few ideas.

1. **Acknowledge your opponent's actions.** Communicate to the other side that in order to reach an agreement both parties will need to be part of this process. Tell them you can't negotiate against yourself and need to hear an offer. If necessary, refuse to answer another question unless you receive a counter-offer.

2. **Call a break.** If you feel that you and your partner are getting antsy or frustrated, call a break yourself. Most competitions allow for each side to have a five-minute break. Don't wait for your opponent to do it. Fix the round yourself by stepping outside and coming up with a plan.

3. **Reframe the conversation.** As the other side continues to prod with more questions, take the opportunity to ask a question yourself: Do you have more questions or can we start to address some of the issues on our agenda?

4. **Remain calm and positive.** You may be screaming on the inside but never let it show. Remain relaxed and positive. Your tone should be abrupt, but you should not cut off the other side. Continue to be positive, but assertive.

Handing Over a Piece of Paper or Agenda

One last tactic to look out for. Most competitions have strict guidelines regarding the use of exhibits or pre-prepared documents. Read the rules carefully, however, because some rules do not prohibit such documents and on occasion teams will bring documents to the negotiation to demonstrate how much they have prepared.

It happens something like this. You shake hands and start to ask your information-gathering questions. Suddenly, your opponent hands you a sheet of paper with their agenda and/or other terms they have mapped out ahead of time and asks you to read it.

Please don't read it. The last thing the judges want to see is a silent table while one side sits and reads a piece of paper. Also, the document rarely adds much to the negotiation. The document tends not to alter the negotiation because it was prepared without the benefit of the other side; therefore, it is biased in favor of the side that prepared it. Instead of sitting and reading the document, acknowledge that you received it, compliment the other side on how great it is, and then continue to proceed in the direction you were going before the team presented you with the document. Don't allow the extra paper to rattle you. You will have prepared a strategy, and you should stick with it.

Quiz Yourself

1. **True or False.** If the opposing team continuously interrupts you or your partner, you should interrupt them as well.

2. **Which of the following are acceptable solutions when the opposing team's behavior is disrespectful?**
   a. Set ground rules for the negotiation.
   b. Speak to the timekeeper about their behavior.
   c. Speak to the judges about their behavior.
   d. Tell the opposing team that the teams need to take a break to think about how the negotiation can proceed.

3. **True of False.** It is never appropriate to walk out of a negotiation.

4. **Which of the following is NOT a good response to the "no offer" tactic?**
   a. Remain calm and positive.
   b. Reframe the conversation.
   c. Acknowledge your opponent's actions.
   d. Threaten the opposing side by saying you will walk out if they do not give you an offer.

5. **True of False:** If your opponent hands you a piece of paper, you should take the time to read it carefully so you can respond effectively to their ideas.

Chapter 11

Negotiation Etiquette

No competition book would be complete without a word about professional appearance. For those of you who are fans of Fashion Police, please keep reading. For those who have no idea who the Fashion Police are, read even closer. At this point, your brain is full of exciting tips and techniques that you are ready to try in your next negotiation, but before you get carried away please remember: nothing speaks louder than your appearance! It is the first thing judges notice, even before you open your mouth. We cannot stress its importance enough. Let me give you a list of some of the most common violations. Men—don't skip this chapter. There is stuff in here for you too.

Short Skirts — No!

Call us old fashioned. We don't mind. But trust us—there is no place for mini-skirts in a negotiation competition. Most of the people who judge the competitions are attorneys and many of them have practiced law longer than you have been alive. Therefore, your attire should be professional and not distracting. It is hard to focus on your arguments when the judges are distracted by your legs. Your skirt should fall at or below your knees. I can see the shock on your face. Someone out there is saying: do they make skirts that long? The answer is YES and you should buy one. Think about this, if your skirt is above the knee when you are standing up, then it will be much higher once you sit down. Very inappropriate. It does not matter how great your legs look, save it for the beach. Pants suits are always an option as well.

Tall Shoes — No!

Stilettos are beautiful and sexy and completely wrong for competition. The goal is to perform the task in a lawyerly fashion. You need a reasonable, conservative, closed toe pump. This is a competition. You may have to walk upstairs and downstairs to various rooms all over the building. The competition usually lasts all day. You want to be comfortable and not tripping around in tall shoes. Stilettos are also visually distracting. You want the judges to be listening to you and not focused on your feet.

The same principle applies to colored shoes. Ladies, don't wear red shoes with your black suit. Gentlemen, avoid the beige shoes or other light (or colored) shoes. Black shoes are beautiful. So are black socks. A negotiation competition is not the time to make a fashion statement.

Tight Clothes — No!

If you are still reading this book, we consider you a friend. As a friend, heed our advice. If you are wearing an outfit — pants, dress, or skirt — and the person behind you can see the outline of your undergarments, it is simply too tight. Go up a size. Nobody knows but you. We will never tell and it looks so much better. This applies to our male readers as well! Tight suits may be the fashion in GQ, but not at the negotiation table.

On the same note, ladies please don't overdo the cleavage. I have seen many competitions where I have had to ask myself: I wonder if she came here straight from the nightclub? Or is she going there right after? You should look like you would if you were going to appear before a judge. Please don't mistake negotiation as a code word for less than professional.

Facial Hair — No!

For our men, this is not the time for the mountain man to try to turn lawyer. Shave it! Some people believe that men with facial hair are trying to hide something. You may not care what those people think on a day to day basis. But, if one of those people happens to be your judge, you may start the negotiation down a point before you have even had the opportunity to speak. Can you think of the last president that has had a beard? I know it sounds odd, but trust us. There is something to a clean face. It sends a message that says I have prepared for this moment. I didn't just roll out of bed. I woke up early and I shaved.

Now is the time for all the excuses and questions. Wait, this goatee looks amazing. My beard is well groomed. Does a mustache count? Stop kidding yourself. Facial hair is facial hair. There are no degrees. The only exception is for cultural or medical reasons. If there is a cultural connection to your facial hair, please keep it. If there is a medical concern, don't shave. Otherwise, get out your razor!

Crayola Colored Suits — No!

If you intend to be a lawyer, you must invest in a dark suit. The suit has to be black or dark navy blue. It is that simple. This applies to you as well ladies. The suit cannot be any other Crayola color — red, green, brown, etc. It cannot be beige. You can attempt gray, but the gray must be so dark that it's charcoal, and if you can get charcoal, you can get black. Plain black is best. A thin (almost non-existent) pin stripe is also okay. No need for the eye-catching thick pin stripes or other patterns.

Your dress shirt should be white. A nice crisp white collared shirt. No blazer and t-shirt craziness. No pocket squares. This is not Miami Vice (Google it if you are too young to know what that is). Lastly, no silly ties. No bow ties. Stick with a traditional tie with a solid or subtle design. A few stripes are fine, but this is not the time to go neon. The goal is to let your words speak for you, not your outfit.

Professional Behavior — Yes!

Okay, so enough about clothes, let's talk about conduct. It should go without saying that your professional behavior should be a constant image that is maintained no matter the circumstances. Competition is no different. You are not judged just when your round starts. Every interaction could be with a competitor, coach, or judge. Mind your manners. Never swear. It is interesting how law students feel so comfortable using colorful language in a professional setting. We are not suggesting you have to be a nun to be successful, but not everybody finds curse words so entertaining or acceptable. Cursing in front of your law professor is not a good thing. Yes, we are all adults and many law professors use more colorful language than students, but it doesn't make it right. Apply the same rules to competition. The competitions are judged by local practitioners. We have had several students offered job opportunities as a result of their performance in competition. Apply the same rules to competition as you would to a job interview.

Anonymity — Yes!

One more thing before we leave the touchy particulars. Some competitions are anonymous, which means the judges do not know where the teams are from. The benefit is that judges will not presume a team is better or worse by what they know about their law school or, more importantly, its ranking. The rule is meant to level the field of competition and limit name bias. If you are in a competition where your school's name is anonymous, keep it that way. Don't tell other teams what school you are from and don't tell the judges. You may even be asked by a judge, "What school are you from?" You still cannot tell them. Politely tell the judge that rules prohibit you from sharing your school's name.

This does not mean you cannot speak with anyone at the competition. It is nice to meet other law students and you can decide if you want to share what school you are from after the competition ends.

Quiz Yourself

1. **True or False:** Judges will not consider your appearance when scoring your negotiation round.

2. **Pick the most appropriate:**
   Skirt above the knee ... or Skirt below the knee?
   Closed toe pump ... or Stilettos?
   Tight clothes ... or Clothes up a size that fit better?
   Beard ... or no beard?
   Neon purple suit ... or Black suit?

3. **When are curse words acceptable?**

4. **True or False.** You should not tell other teams what school you are from, but you are permitted to tell the judges.

5. **True or False.** It is always better to wear bright colors so judges will remember you.

Chapter 12

 **Self-Evaluation**

Believe it or not, this may be the most important chapter in this book. Many times rounds at the competition are so close that judges have a hard time deciding which team should advance. After the self-evaluation, the choice becomes quite obvious. Mastering the self-evaluation is critical because it may become the determining factor as to whether you advance or go home.

What Is a Self-Evaluation?

Following the negotiation round, each team is asked to evaluate their performance at the table. At this point, both teams leave the room and have a set period of time to prepare an evaluation. Typically, the teams are given ten minutes to prepare. After the ten minutes are complete, one of the teams will be asked to return to the room and reflect on the round. Once that team is finished, the other team will enter the room and provide their reflection of the round.

The rules of the competition will provide guidance as to what should be discussed during the self-evaluation. Several competitions ask the students to answer the following two questions: (i) If you were to do the same negotiation tomorrow, what would you do the same and what would you do differently; and (ii) how did your strategy work with respect to your overall outcome?

Each team usually has ten minutes to answer these questions. During the ten-minute self-evaluation, the judges can sit quietly and listen to the reflection, or the judges can interrupt the competitors to ask questions. The questions will vary from round to round. A judge could ask you why your initial offer was so extreme. A judge could ask whether you thought you were cooperative or adversarial. We have heard questions about strategy, the agenda, interaction with the other team, etc. There truly is no question off the table and you have to be able to respond effectively to any question asked.

Remember the self-evaluation is often the most critical part of the competition. Often both teams are very effective at the table and it is not until the self-evaluation that a true winner emerges. Thus, always practice your self-evaluation before competition and take it very seriously while you are at competition. Following are our top ten tips on how to make your self-evaluation the best possible.

Top Ten Tips for an Effective Self-Evaluation

1. **Introduce yourself before you start.** Before you begin your self-evaluation, each member of the team should introduce themselves to the judges and one of the team members should tell the judges: (i) what your team number/name is; and (ii) which party your team represented.

2. **Answer the questions posed to you by the competition.** The rules of each competition will provide you with guidance on what you should reflect upon in your self-evaluation. The topics mentioned above are typical, but the topics can vary from competition to competition. Make sure you reflect on the topics set forth for your particular competition.

Be careful to use the exact wording provided in the topics provided. The judges will be told what topics you should reflect upon and if you change the wording of the topics, you risk a judge thinking you missed a topic. For example, if the competition asks you to reflect on what you would do the same and what you would do differently, you should actually say, "If we were to do the same negotiation tomorrow, there are three things we would do differently." Then follow that statement with details on what you would change.

3. **Discuss each category on the score sheet.** In responding to the self-evaluation topics provided, you should keep in mind what categories the judges will be scoring you on. For example, if one of the categories on the score sheet is flexibility, you should mention somewhere in your self-evaluation that you were flexible and give specific examples of your flexibility. If the score sheet asks the judges to score you on teamwork, you should explain to the judges why your teamwork was effective. Following your self-evaluation, the judges will score you on these categories and you want the judge to remember how effective you were for each as they decide what score to give you.

4. **Be reflective.** Use your preparation time for your self-evaluation to truly reflect on your round. A good self-evaluation goes further than "we could have used our time more wisely" or "we shouldn't have interrupted each other." Although these responses are fine, they result in a "fine" self-evaluation. You need to do better than "fine." Really think about what the judges would want you to change. If you are able to discuss things the judges thought were ineffective, you have nailed the self-evaluation. Also, you should not only mention the things that you would change, but explain how your change would have affected the round. For example, instead of just saying, "We started with a number that was too high," explain how starting with a lower number would have changed the round.

5. **Don't be too negative.** Be careful not to beat yourself up too badly during the self-evaluation. Although you want to be reflective, you also need to remember that the self-evaluation is a sales pitch. It is your chance to convince your judges that you should win. Include things that could have gone better, but keep your overall tone positive. Also, think carefully about what you confess could have gone better. You never want to say things like "The other side had control of the negotiation" or "we didn't listen to the other side." Ability to control the table and the ability to listen to the other team are too critical to being an effective negotiator. If your self-evaluation says the other team had control of the round, you just asked to be ranked last. The things you could change should be more specific, such as, "we should have started with issue one first because it would have gained us momentum by the time we got to issue three."

6. **Emphasize your outcome.** Make sure you have a place in your self-evaluation where you sell your outcome to the judges. In several competitions, the outcome score serves as a tie-breaker. In fact, we once won a competition based solely on our outcome score. Thus, you need to convince the judges you got a great deal for your client. If you really convince the judges how happy your client would be with the deal, you are likely to score higher in that category. It may be the difference between advancing or going home. As you describe the outcome to the judges, you should link each item negotiated to the client's goals. Make sure to highlight how much in excess of your client's goals you achieved. For example, "Our client wanted $20,000 in compensation and we got him $32,000 — $12,000 more than he was hoping to achieve."

7. **Don't criticize the other team.** A self-evaluation is exactly that. An evaluation of yourself. Making negative remarks about the opposing team is never appropriate. This holds true even if the opposing side was rude, interrupted you, did not understand the problem, or was just plain ineffective. Instead of saying the other side did something wrong, talk about how you effectively used your skills to move the negotiation forward.

You should also avoid complimenting the other team. You want to win. Telling the judges that the other team was really effective does not help you win. Keep your evaluation focused on your team: what you did well and what you can improve upon.

8. **Share the time equally with your partner.** Just as teamwork during the round is important, teamwork during the self-evaluation is important. You and your partner should talk equally during your self-evaluation and you should both be active during the entire evaluation. Rather than having one partner speak for the first half and the other partner speak for the second half, try to divide the self-evaluation topics up such that you are both actively involved the entire time. Perhaps one team member talks about what you would do differently and the other talks about what you would keep the same. Then the first team member talks about your outcome and the other the next topic, etc.

9. **Be ready for questions.** Some judges will just stare at you during self-evaluation and never say a word. Some judges will wait to

until the end of the self-evaluation to ask you questions. Some judges will cut you off in the middle of a sentence and ask you a question. Regardless of which judge you have, you need to be ready to answer any questions that come up. There are a few rules to keep in mind.

Rule 1: You can never interrupt a judge. If a judge is asking a long-winded question and you know exactly what the judge is trying to ask, stay quiet until the judge is finished speaking. If a judge is asking you a series of questions and you are getting overwhelmed, stay quiet until the judge is finished speaking. If a judge is accusing you of doing something you did not do, stay quiet until the judge is finished speaking. You will have your chance to respond; remember to be patient.

Rule 2: The judge is always right. Perhaps a judge tells you "Don't you think it would have been better to start with a lower number?" Perhaps you think, "Heck no!" Your answer is "Yes." Tell the judge that you planned to start high because you were hoping it would yield a higher return; however, in retrospect you can see how the number may have had an adverse effect on the negotiation. You never want to argue with a judge. Your job is to get the judge to like you. Telling the judges they are wrong will not get the judges to like you. At the same time, you want to explain why you thought your strategy was effective. Thus, be respectful, say what you think the judge wants to hear, but also try to get an explanation in of why you approached the problem in the way you did.

Rule 3: Answer the question asked. Listen carefully to what the judge is asking. If you don't understand the question, ask the judge to repeat or clarify. Be careful that your answer is actually addressing what the judge is asking and you are not rambling about something you want the judges to hear.

10. **Be yourself.** The self-evaluation is your chance to get the judge to like you. If both teams at the table are strong, the judge will pick a winner based on your personalities. Let your personality shine. Be relaxed. Be friendly. Be professional. Avoid being too stiff or too formal. Ultimately, try to let the judges see who you really are and, assuming you are a likeable person, the self-evaluation will help you win the round.

Quiz Yourself

1. **True or False.** The self-evaluation is often the most critical part of the competition.

2. **True or False.** You should use the score sheet as a guide for the topics to cover in your self-evaluation.

3. **True or False:** In a self-evaluation, you should avoid discussing things you could improve on because you don't want to acknowledge your mistakes in front of the judges.

4. **True or False:** A good self-evaluation sets forth not only your weaknesses, but the weakness of the opposing team.

5. **Which of the following are appropriate during the question and answer part of the self-evaluation?**
   a. If a judge asks you a question in the middle of your planned self-evaluation, you should politely tell the judge you will answer the question at the end of your planned speech.
   b. Interrupt a judge only when the judge is asking multiple questions at one time.
   c. Answer the specific question asked of you.
   d. Respond as if the judges are always right.

Chapter 13

Scoring and Ranking the Teams

So, you have followed all the tips in this book. Now the big question, how do you win? Every competition sets its own rules on how to advance in a competition, but a common approach has emerged for most competitions.

Typically, a panel of three judges observes your round. Each judge will see four teams and rank the teams 1–4. In addition, each judge will fill out a score sheet for each team. Details about each of these methods follows.

Ranking System

The panel of judges in each room will see two teams negotiate against each other. When the first two teams finish their negotiation, two more teams will come in the room in front of the same judges and do a negotiation on the same problem. After the judges have watched all four teams, each judge will rank the four teams from best (1) to worst (4). Ideally, all three of your judges will think you were the best of the four teams. If this occurs, all three judges will rank you first and you will have a total score of three. This is the best score you can receive and you will definitely advance to the next round.

A score of all "ones" is not typical, however. The judges do not always agree about which team was best. We have seen judges give one team a one and another judge give that same team a four. Negotiation is subjective. Although there are some generally accepted negotiation principles, each judge bases the ranking on the judge's own personal experience with negotiation. Your job is to please most of the judges most the time. If you get a mixture of "ones" and "twos," you are likely to advance. Even a mixture of "ones" and "threes" or sometimes even "twos" and "threes" will be enough to get you to the next round.

Our tips in this book are geared toward getting most of the judges to like you the best. If you try unorthodox negotiation tactics, you may get one judge who absolutely loves you, but you risk the other judges thinking your strategy was ineffective. It is best to play it safe. Aim for all "ones," but remember "twos" will usually do the job. From our experience, having a solid strategy and good negotiation techniques will get you much further than trying to use ploys and tactics to disrupt the other team.

Score Sheets

In addition to ranking the four teams, each judge will fill out a score sheet for each team. A typical score sheet asks the judges to score the teams in the following categories: preparation, strategy, flexibility, outcome, teamwork, self-evaluation, and ethics.

In the preparation category, judges will score you on how well you knew the facts of the problem and how well you prepared to present arguments and justifications for your client as well as respond to arguments from opposing counsel.

In the strategy category, judges will score you based on how you approached the problem and whether your strategy was effective. The judges will consider your negotiation style (adversarial v. cooperative), as well as your general approach to addressing the issues.

In the flexibility category, judges will score you on how well you were able to adapt and change your plan as the negotiation progressed. The judges will consider whether you were flexible in addressing the issues, whether you were flexible in accepting terms from the other side, and whether you could adapt your strategy based on the information you obtained during the round.

In the outcome category, the judges will score you based on the terms of the deal you reached. If you settle at your bottom line, your deal will not get as high a score as if you got the other side to move to their bottom line. However, you can receive a high outcome score even if you did not finalize a deal. If your progression in the round suggested you were headed in the direction of a great deal, a judge can still score you well in this category. This category is the most important on the score sheet because it can become the basis of a tie-breaker (discussed below).

In the teamwork category, the judges score you based on your teamwork with your partner as well as your teamwork with opposing counsel. The judges will consider whether both members of a team contributed equally to the round. They will also consider whether the members of the team worked as a cohesive group rather than two individuals sitting on the same side of the table. If the members of team continuously interrupt each other or fail to support each other's ideas, the score is likely to be low. In judging your teamwork with opposing counsel, the judges will consider whether your interactions with the other side furthered an agreement or precluded an agreement. The judges are looking to see if you are respectful of the other side and willing to listen and address the opposing side's concerns.

In the self-evaluation category, the judges score you based on how reflective you were about your performance. If you were thoughtful, reflective, and organized you are likely to receive a high score. If you fail to mention anything that could be improved, argue with the judges, or lack structure in your presentation, your score will be lower.

In the ethics category, the judges will consider whether you made any misrepresentations of fact or created other ethical concerns. During competition, you are not permitted to misrepresent any of the facts provided to you in the negotiation problem. This includes misrepresenting how much or how little your client is willing to pay. If your client is willing to pay $10,000 to resolve a dispute, you are not permitted to tell opposing counsel, "My client can't pay

"$9,000," Although such bluffing may be permissible in real practice, it is frowned upon in the competition environment. Although misrepresentations of fact are the most common ethical violations, other ethical concerns can also arise based on the specific facts of the problem.

Typically, the score sheet only comes into play when there is tie between two teams. However, in some competitions the winners are chosen based solely on the total score from the score sheets.

Tie Breakers

If the judges' ranking results in the same score for two teams, the team that has the highest total score on the score sheet after adding the scores in all categories together, will advance. If there is still a tie, the highest score under "outcome" will usually advance.

We once tied for first place in the final round. There was a panel of four judges watching the round. Two judges ranked our team first and our opponent second. Two judges ranked our opponent first and our team second. Each team thus had a total of six points. The host of the competition then looked at the total points received on the score sheets. The teams were still tied. Next was the outcome score. We won. Most of the judges thought our outcome was better. Thus, we took home the trophy. It can really be this close.

At another competition, the tie breaker actually came down to a coin toss. After looking at all the tie breaking procedures, our team was still tied. The only option left was for the host to flip a coin to see who advanced. Always pick heads!

There are a variety of tie-breaking procedures among the competitions. Southwestern uses a unique tie-breaking procedure at the Entertainment Negotiation Competition. Southwestern looks at the rankings of the judges. After adding up the total ranking scores, if two teams are tied, the team that received the most "ones" advances. If both teams received an equal number of ones, the team that received the most "twos" advances, and so forth.

Always look at the rules for your competition before you compete so you know the tie-breaking procedures.

Appeals and Challenges

You should also check your rules for the policies regarding appeals or challenges. Know the procedure for appealing a decision before you show up to the competition. When you check-in at the competition, find out who the person in charge of the competition is so you know who to talk to if you encounter a problem during one of your rounds.

Before making any complaint, however, you should speak to your faculty advisor. Multiple complaints from a school, especially when the complaints are minor, can harm the school's reputation. You must go into the competition understanding that the process is subjective, mistakes happen, and the learning process is what ultimately matters. Don't get upset over small things that don't go your way. Very rarely will any complaints change an outcome. Rather, they will merely tarnish your reputation. Make a complaint only when there is a clear and severe breach of the rules (i.e. your judge was your opponent's mom).

Chapter 14

Other Types of ADR Competitions

The basic framework we have discussed so far involves the traditional negotiation competition. There are a variety of negotiation competitions across the nation. The American Bar Association is currently the competition with the largest number of competitors. Each year, the ABA selects a topic for the competition. Topics could cover any field of law from Employment Law to Estate Planning. The ABA divides the schools into regions based on the geographic location of the school and each region has a regional competition. Teams who advance from the regional competition compete at the national competition, which usually takes place during the ABA midyear meeting. The ABA regional competition allows for students to negotiate two preliminary rounds and then the top four teams advance to the final round.

In addition to the ABA competition, various schools have started hosting their own negotiation competitions. Thomas Jefferson Law School hosts a Sports Law competition. Liberty Law School, Fordham Law School, South Texas School of Law, and Richmond School of Law also have their own negotiation competitions. Competitions are changing constantly. A quick Google search for "law school negotiation competitions" should get you headed in the right direction.

In addition to the traditional negotiation competitions, a variety of variations have emerged giving students an opportunity to display different, but related skills. These include mediation competitions, arbitration competitions, drafting competitions, and client counseling competitions.

Mediation Competitions

Mediation competitions have expanded in number over the last decade. In mediation competitions, the number of competitors on a team may vary depending on the competition. Some competitions have a two-person team where one plays the role of client and the other plays the role of lawyer. Other competitions have three-person teams where one student plays the role of mediator, one plays the role of lawyer, and one plays the role of client. In some competitions, students are required to submit a mediation planning memorandum to the judges. The memorandum documents the parties' positions as they enter the mediation and what they hope to accomplish.

In mediation competitions, students are assessed on their ability to advocate for their client during the mediation. Judges will critique students on how effectively they use the mediator, how effectively they advocate for their client's interests, and how effectively they facilitate a solution. The focus in mediation competitions is slightly different from the focus in negotiation competitions. Mediation, by definition, is a facilitated negotiation. The mediator changes the dynamic of the round. These competitions still have general facts and confidential facts for each side. In mediation competitions, however, there is a neutral third party present (i.e., the mediator). The mediator's role is to encourage the parties to reach an agreement.

The American Bar Association also has Advocacy in Mediation Competition that is run similar to the Negotiation Competition, with regional meets and a national meet. Osgood Hall also sponsors an International Mediation Competition each year in Toronto. Teams participate in three preliminary rounds, with the top eight teams advancing to the semifinals, and the top four advancing to the final round.

Arbitration Competitions

Arbitration is the form of ADR that most closely resembles litigation. In arbitration, the parties prepare opening and closing statements. There is the opportunity to examine a limited number of witnesses and review a limited amount of evidence in preparation for the hearing. The main distinction that arbitration has from other forms of dispute resolution, however, is that an arbitrator actually makes a decision about who is right and who is wrong. Whereas negotiation and mediation are voluntary non-binding processes, a neutral third party picks a winner of the arbitrated case. For competition purposes, it is important to note the distinction in the process. It is also important to note the skills tested. Whereas mediation and negotiation focus on problem solving skills and the ability to compromise, arbitration's focus is about opening and closing statements and questioning of witnesses.

The American Bar Association also hosts an Arbitration competition. The competition is administered in a similar fashion to the negotiation competition. There are regional rounds depending on the school's location and the winners advance to a national round.

Drafting Competitions

Another twist to negotiation competitions has been the addition of drafting contracts or term sheets. There are a few competitions that incorporate a writing component to the competition. Students still have a set of general facts and confidential instructions from their client, but students also have a video of their client and other relevant documents that provide the content for the term sheet the students are expected to create.

Most of the drafting competitions are structured to allow the teams to exchange drafts of their written work before the negotiation. The preparation for these types of competition is usually more extensive because they provide a large volume of information in order to give students the background to draft an agreement.

Drexel has created an innovative competition that involves drafting a term sheet before meeting to negotiate the deal. Teams exchange their term sheet with both of the teams they will face in the competition. Thus, the process resembles real world practice because teams can prepare for the negotiation knowing ahead of time what the other side is looking to achieve. USC School of Law recently added a similar drafting competition.

Attorney/Client Negotiation Competitions

Recently, a new competition has become popular where each team plays the role of attorney and client. In traditional negotiation competitions, all four competitors play the role of attorneys. In the attorney/client competition, one student from each side is asked to be counsel and the other student on the team is asked to be the client. This new format presents an interesting change in the dichotomy between the teams and between the individuals representing one side.

First, the student playing the client must play the role of that client and not act like an attorney. The client is usually someone outside the legal field. As such, the client must act the part of someone who does not know the law. For example, assume one team is asked to represent a collegiate student athlete suing for concussions he sustained while playing football. One of the students on the team must play the role of the attorney representing the athlete and the other student must play the role of the football player himself. The athlete-client should not come across as a legal expert and should not make legal arguments. He has to draw on emotion and really become the character he was asked to be. He should act like an injured football player.

Second, the attorneys must be careful not to address their opposing counsel's client sitting across the table. An attorney is not permitted to speak directly to a client who is represented by counsel. Thus, the attorney on one side of the table must address the attorney on the opposing side and be careful not to specifically ask questions directly to the opposing side's client.

Client Counseling Competitions

A large part of what we do as lawyers is giving advice; however, very few law schools actually educate students on how to communicate with clients in a language the clients will understand. Client counseling competitions provide students the opportunity to play the role of a lawyer giving advice to a potential client during a client intake interview. At the competition, students interview the client in pairs. The students are not aware ahead of time what legal problem the client has or any specifics regarding why the client is seeking legal advice. Students are only given a sheet of paper with one or two sentences about the client. For example,

> *Ms. Catherine Brown has come to see you today about a disagreement she is having with her neighbor.*

With this limited amount of information, students are faced with the challenge of interviewing the client and finding out what the legal and non-legal concerns are for the client and also with giving the client legal options. At the end of the interviewing session, the students escort the client to the door and have a meeting between themselves in front of the judges about what the next course of action should be. The judges evaluate students on how well they connect with the client, whether the students asked effective questions, whether the students gave the client several options, and whether the students have a good plan for how to assist the client.

The American Bar Association Law Student Division has regional and national client counseling competitions annually.

Appendix A

Sample Negotiation Problem with Example Negotiation Plans

General Facts
D.O.G.
By Ashley Miller

Arnold and Betty live in a small apartment complex on the north side of Apple road. They own a golden retriever named D.O.G. They often walk D.O.G. along Apple road in the morning, afternoon, and evenings. D.O.G is very well behaved and is friendly to all the people she encounters on her walks with Arnold and Betty. She was rescued from the humane society 5 years ago, where she was dropped off by her abusive owner and separated from her mother when she was just 3 months old. Arnold and Betty take great care of her and she is a kind natured golden retriever, known as one of the nicest dogs in the neighborhood.

On the afternoon of August 23, Arnold and Betty took D.O.G. out for a walk. As part of their routine, they let D.O.G. off the leash for a few minutes to run around in front of their apartment. During this time, a speeding car, blaring its horn and music went by and startled D.O.G. She quickly took off running to get away from the car. Arnold and Betty looked everywhere for her. They asked all the neighbors in the apartment complex to keep an eye out for her. They posted posters all over the neighborhood. When they realized they had been searching for hours, they decided to go inside and take a break, hoping that she would come back to the apartment complex. They were devastated and worried that she may never come back. All they could think about was that they hoped she was okay and uninjured.

Calvin was the 19-year-old boy who had been driving the speeding car that startled D.O.G. When he got back home that evening he parked in his usual spot under the carport, but the motion sensor light did not turn on. As he walked to his apartment, an animal approached him. Calvin claims that the next thing he knew, the animal in the dark had bitten him. Calvin knew that Arnold and Betty's dog had been missing because they had asked him to keep an eye out for her. Since he knew that she was on the loose, he believed that the animal that bit him was D.O.G. This was a horrible experience for Calvin because as a child a dog had attacked him and he was always wary of them from then on. Calvin had been tolerant of D.O.G. because Arnold and Betty had assured him that she was a sweet dog that could never harm anyone, but he no longer feels that way. He does not want to feel as though there is a dangerous dog running around the neighborhood and after this incident he is thinking that D.O.G. is a dangerous dog.

Arnold and Betty woke up the morning after D.O.G. disappeared to find him sitting peacefully on their porch. The parties live in Westmoreland, Wilshire. The following is the only law on point:

Section 22.4 Dog Bite Law:

If a vicious dog bites a person, the dog must be euthanized unless the person who was bitten agrees the dog need not be euthanized. The owner of the dog is liable for all damages incurred as a result of the dog's actions.

Arnold and Betty Confidential Facts:

Arnold and Betty know that while their dog is generally very calm and not aggressive. However, when provoked by a male, D.O.G. has been known to growl and get close to a person in a threatening manner. D.O.G. has never bitten anyone, but she has scared people on a few occasions, including one month ago when she jumped aggressively at Arnold's cousin who had come over to visit.

Since the bite incident occurred, Arnold and Betty have been very concerned about what is going to happen to their beloved dog.

Arnold and Betty see D.O.G. like a child to them. She goes with them everywhere and they had her since she was a little puppy.

While Arnold and Betty don't feel that this is an incident that is likely to occur again, they want to make sure that nothing bad is going to happen to D.O.G. They are worried about the dog bite law and absolutely do not want to put D.O.G. down. While they are skeptical that Calvin would be able to meet all the elements of the law, they do not want to risk litigation and having it fall in favor of Calvin. Ideally, they could convince Calvin that D.O.G. is not a dangerous dog and if it was her that bit him, it was a one-time occurrence that will not happen again so she should get another chance and nothing should happen to her. However, they understand that being bit by a dog is traumatizing, so they are willing to enroll D.O.G. in some type of training program. The City of Westmoreland offers a dog training program for $120 for a six-week session. It meets once a week and has glowing reviews. Ideally, Calvin will agree to this; however, you are ultimately willing to agree to whatever class/training is necessary to appease Calvin. Negotiate the least expensive, least restrictive option you can.

Arnold and Betty know that Calvin is going to want his medical expenses paid. They understand this request, but because they are still skeptical of the situation and want to try to talk him out of the medical expenses because he doesn't have proof it was D.O.G. However, they are willing to pay up to $7,000 in medical expenses, if necessary and Calvin provides a copy of the medical bills. If necessary, Arnold and Betty are also willing to offer him up to $2,000 in pain and suffering, but they prefer not to pay any pain and suffering especially since they don't even know that it was D.O.G. that attacked him.

Additionally, Arnold and Betty want to make sure that if they are paying all this money to Calvin, they don't have to worry about the next time they take D.O.G. outside. They want to continue taking her out in the same manner they had before, allowing her to be free to roam around the area right in front of their home with supervision. If she does go into a type of training, they think it is incredibly fair because already being a calm natured golden retriever who has undergone training would make her an extremely well-behaved dog. However, Arnold and Betty know that in order to make sure D.O.G is going to continue to be their dog, they may have to sacrifice their usual routine. Thus, they will agree to keep D.O.G. on a leash in the apartment complex at all times until she finishes her training, with the hopes that when she finishes training Calvin will feel safe enough that she can again play without a leash when supervised. If Calvin feels uncomfortable because of the incident still, they are willing to have her on a leash anytime they are out of the house and they will carry a muzzle with them to put on her if she seems to be getting aggressive or if Calvin is around. However, they feel muzzles are mean to the animal and would like you to push on this.

The most important thing for Arnold and Betty is to make sure that D.O.G. can continue to live a long and happy life with them and they hope that you can come to an agreement with Calvin about the future of their beloved D.O.G.

Calvin Confidential Facts:

Calvin does not like dogs. He has hoped to have the neighbors get rid of their dog since he moved in. Dogs have always made Calvin uncomfortable from when he was young. His brother had an aggressive dog that always growled, barked, and once bit Calvin, so he prefers to avoid dogs at all costs. However, this is Westmoreland, and everyone loves dogs, so he has had to continue to deal with them.

The night the incident occurred, it was very dark and Calvin was tired. Usually the parking area of his apartment has a motion sensor, but the light did not come on. As he walked towards the door a furry animal ran up to him. Unsure of whether the animal was approaching him in an aggressive manner, he began to shout at it to try to scare it off. The animal ran up to him and bit him on the leg. He does not actually know whether it was D.O.G. or another animal that bit him, but the animal did look about the size of a golden retriever and he knows that earlier that day Arnold and Betty had been out looking for D.O.G.

Immediately after the bite, Calvin went to the hospital. The doctor told him the bite was not bad, but he would still need to stay at the hospital to have the wound treated, stitches, and a series of immunizations to ensure no disease or infection would occur. Calvin does not have medical insurance and the total cost of the hospital visit was $8,000. Calvin wants Arnold and Betty to pay for this expense. If they are not willing to pay the full amount, he would like them to pay for at least half of the medical expenses. He does not feel like he should have to pay for an incident that could likely have been prevented. He is willing to show them medical bills if necessary to secure payment.

Additionally, Calvin would like to ask for pain and suffering damages. He is hoping to get $5,000 but recognizes that might not be realistic. Try to get the maximum amount that they are willing to offer.

Calvin feels the dog bite law is in his favor. Due to his experience with dogs as a child and his incident adding to his trauma, he feels that D.O.G. should be put down. If Arnold and Betty feel this is too severe, Calvin is willing to negotiate another option. Perhaps D.O.G. is enrolled in a dog aggression-training course or comparable training program. Calvin would like to have final say on the course because he wants it to be one that will help to alleviate his fear if he runs into D.O.G. again. There is a specific course that Calvin has in mind. It is an intensive training course for aggressive dogs. It is offered by a company called "We Stop the Aggression." Calvin is hoping D.O.G. will be enrolled in the 8 week course that meets three times a week. It is expensive (about $1,000), but he will feel safest with the most training possible. There is an even more intensive course for $5,000 where the dog stays at the We Stop Aggression Center for two weeks with daily visits from its owners, but he is not requiring that. He is trying to be reasonable. If necessary, Calvin will agree to a less intensive course as long as it is offered by We Stop the Aggression. There are several 8 week courses to choose from varying from 1 day per week ($500), 2 days per week ($800), 3 days per week ($1,000) and 5 days per week ($1300). Each training session is one hour and is offered at various times throughout the day/night.

Finally, Calvin wants D.O.G. to wear a muzzle when out of the house. This includes any place in Westmoreland. Dog Parks, Petco, beaches, etc. He is willing to make the muzzle requirement only in the neighborhood if necessary and will also agree to remove the restriction after the end of the training program if necessary. However, Arnold and Betty must agree that D.O.G. will always be on a leash when he is in the neighborhood (even after he has completed the training program).

Example Negotiation Plan:
Arnold & Betty

Introduction: Your theme for your introduction should focus on the idea that D.O.G. is a rescued golden retriever who is now part of Arnold's and Betty's family. In your introduction, make Arnold and Betty look like saints for adopting D.O.G. and emphasize all facts that demonstrate how much D.O.G. is loved and any facts that show he is not dangerous. Remember that when you are done with the introduction, someone who did not read the facts should understand a basic summary of what happened.

Information Gathering Question: It is critical in this negotiation to find out what evidence Calvin has that D.O.G. actually bit him. Approach the question in this way: "Arnold and Betty are shocked that Calvin thinks D.O.G. is the animal that attacked him. They have been told it was dark at the time of the incident and that Calvin could not see the animal that bit him. Arnold and Betty think it is possible a different animal actually bit Calvin. Does Calvin have any evidence that D.O.G. is the animal that bit him?"

Agenda:
1. Training Program (to alleviate any fear by Calvin that D.O.G. is dangerous)
2. Restraint of D.O.G. until training program is over.

[Do not include compensation on the agenda because Arnold and Betty want to avoid monetary payment if possible.]

Outline of Arnold's and Betty's interests:
- **Training:**
  - Ideally D.O.G. will attend the City's six-week program for $120.
  - Bottom line: Arnold and Betty are willing to do any training program to avoid litigation—try to get the least expensive and least restrictive program possible.
- **Restraining D.O.G.**
  - Ideally D.O.G. will only have to be on a leash until the training course is over.

- Bottom line: Arnold and Betty are willing to keep D.O.G. on a leash and in a muzzle while in the neighborhood.

- **Compensation**
  - Ideally Arnold and Betty would like to avoid paying any money to Calvin
  - Bottom line: willing to pay 9,000 total (7,000 in medical bills and 2,000 pain and suffering); Calvin must show proof of medical costs.

Example Negotiation Plan:
Calvin

Introduction: Your theme for the negotiation should focus on the idea that although Calvin understands how much D.O.G. means to Arnold and Betty, D.O.G. is dangerous and it is too risky to put another's life in danger regardless of how much he is loved. Remember that when you are done with the introduction, someone who did not read the facts should understand a basic summary of what happened.

*Note: You must be very careful how you approach the introduction and all issues in the negotiation as a whole. It is very easy to offend someone who is an animal enthusiast by failing to choose your words and tone carefully. Be aware your judge may have a deeply loved dog at home and you must avoid saying anything that would sound heartless or cold.

Information Gathering Question: Are Arnold and Betty aware of any instance where D.O.G. has shown aggression in the past?

Agenda:
1. Compensation for Calvin's injuries;
2. Avoiding future attacks by D.O.G.

[When you discuss the second agenda item, you should first suggest D.O.G. be put down to avoid risk of future attack, but you should be willing to quickly move from that to the training and restraint of D.O.G. You don't want to list training and restraint of D.O.G. as separate categories in your agenda because if you include those items on the agenda, it will indicate you do not really need D.O.G. to be put down.]

Outline of Calvin's interests:
- **Compensation:**
    - Ideally Calvin would like $13,000 ($8,000 for medical expenses and $5,000 for pain and suffering)
    - Bottom line: Calvin is willing to settle for as little as $4,000 total if necessary.

- **Training for D.O.G.**
  - Ideally D.O.G. will attend the 8 week course by "We Stop the Aggression" for $1,000.
  - Bottom line: Calvin will settle as long as D.O.G. attends one of the courses offered by "We Stop the Aggression."
- **Restraint of D.O.G.**
  - Ideally, Calvin would like Arnold and Betty to keep D.O.G. on a leash and in a muzzle anytime D.O.G. goes outside the house—even to the beach, etc.
  - Bottom line: Calvin will agree to settle so long as D.O.G. wears a muzzle and leash while in the neighborhood until the training is complete and on a leash while in the neighborhood after the training is complete.

Appendix B

Additional Negotiation Problem: Low Difficulty

General Information
Phil & Joe
By Cristina Knolton

Phil and Joe are brothers. They grew up in Mission Hills, Westmoreland, in a beautiful 800-square-foot home that sits on two acres of land. The home was small but perfect for their family. Phil, the older of the two sons, has lived with his parents his entire life. Even after his mother died, he stayed at home to help his dad. Joe, the baby of the family, was more independent. When Joe turned eighteen he moved to Florida and has lived there ever since. He has lost touch with his brother, but does call home once or twice a year to check in on his dad.

Last month, Mo passed away. In his will, Mo left his entire estate to Phil. The will was dated January 20, 1980, one year before Joe was born. Mo's estate consists of the family home and a $100,000 bank account. The brothers are now in a dispute as to who is entitled to the assets.

The following law applies:

Westmoreland Probate Code Section 21620. If a will fails to provide for a child of the decedent born after the execution of the will, the omitted child shall receive a share of the estate equal to all other children provided for in the will unless the other children can show the decedent would not have intended the omitted child to share in the estate.

Confidential Facts for Phil's Attorney

Phil is very upset. He was very close to his father and is having trouble coping with his loss. The only thing he has left is the family home. It reminds him of his parents and everything he loved about his childhood. He wants nothing more than to continue living in the home. He hopes one day he can raise his own children in the home.

He doesn't think his brother has much of a case. After all, his father's will clearly provides that Phil will receive all the property and his father certainly intended it that way. Joe never really fit into the family. He always wanted to get away and as soon as he had the chance he moved as far away as he could. He has not visited his parents in over ten years. There is no way Mo would want Joe to have an interest in this home.

However, Phil is worried. If Joe does get an interest in the house, the first thing Joe will do is petition the court to sell the home so he can get his profit. He has always been greedy in that way. Thus, to avoid losing the chance to raise his children in his childhood home, Phil is willing to do everything in his power. He will give Joe the $100,000 bank account in full if Joe will walk away quietly. Given the home is only worth $100,000, that is an even split — the best Joe will ever get even if this were taken to court. If Joe is stubborn and won't take the $100,000, Phil is willing to do anything he can to keep the home. Phil is a successful businessman and has a hefty bank account. He is willing to pay Joe his entire life savings if necessary just to get ownership of the house. His bank account has $50,000 — try to promise as little as possible to get the house.

Confidential Facts for Joe's Attorney

Joe is mad. He can't believe his big brother is trying to pull one over on him again. Phil has always been the brother that has to be the best and has always done his best to exclude Joe. Joe couldn't wait to get out of the house once he had the chance. Since then he has done his best to keep in touch with his parents. Life just gets busy. He calls them every year on their birthday (they share the same birthday). He avoids visiting because being around Phil just makes things worse.

Joe knows his dad loved him and would want to care for him in the same way he did Phil. He just never modified the old will since Joe was born. Thus, Joe thinks he has a strong case if he brought this to court.

However, he can't risk the loss. Joe has done a lot of research on the family home over the years and has discovered there are valuable minerals underground. Although the property value of the home is only known to be about $100,000—with the potential mineral rights below it is easily worth at least four times that amount. Joe wants to make sure he gets his share. Thus, he wants you to secure an agreement with his brother that gives him equal interest in the property in addition to half the money in the bank account. If Phil will not agree to this arrangement, Joe will settle for just the interest in the property. This will ultimately result in plenty of money. If he can get an equal interest in the property, he can convince a court to order a sale of the property. With the research he has performed, he is confident he can sell the property for at least $400,000, leaving him with $200,000 profit.

Appendix C

Additional Negotiation Problem: Average Difficulty

General Facts
Tomcat v. LVP
By Nathan Brogden

Tomcat is an American men's lifestyle and entertainment magazine founded in the state of Westmoreland in 1953 by Lou Fefner and his associates. Notable for its centerfolds of nude and seminude models, Tomcat played an important role in the sexual revolution and remains one of the world's best known brands, having grown into Tomcat Enterprises, Inc., with a presence in nearly every medium. In addition to the flagship magazine in the United States, nation-specific versions of Tomcat are published globally.

Tomcat's market value is estimated to be in the neighborhood of $400 million, much of which has been accredited to astute business decisions on the part of its newest board of directors (the "Board"). In November of 2012, the Board decided to branch out into other, non-media sectors of the marketplace and create a vodka brand bearing its own trademark to sell to the public. Because of Tomcat's lack of expertise in such matters, the Board acknowledged that they would need to hire a licensing agency to identify the best vodka manufacturer possible. Tomcat wanted to be sure they had the best product available to uphold the high standards they have already established through their other business endeavors. To that end, Tomcat approached LVP, Inc., a licensing agency, in December of 2012, with the proposition of a mutually beneficial partnership between the two companies. LVP, Inc. ("LVP") was excited about the opportunity to work with a brand whose name already carried such great weight worldwide. LVP takes an incredible amount of pride in its ability to find the perfect match between a brand and a manufacturer of fine spirits. Because of their highly skilled employees and wide-reach within the alcohol industry, LVP has come to be known as the absolute best in the business. LVP believed that, because of the "party nature" of Tomcat's established brand, an expansion into the liquor industry would be a natural fit and an extremely profitable venture.

After much negotiation, Tomcat and LVP were able to reach a three-year exclusive license agreement. Tomcat agreed to pay LVP a license fee of $9 million, to be paid in three installments: 1/3 upon execution of the agreement, 1/3 upon the completion of the first year of the agreement, and 1/3 upon the completion of the second year of the agreement. Tomcat also agreed to give LVP a royalty of 10% from all of Tomcat's vodka net profits during the term of the agreement. LVP promised to use its best efforts to find opportunities to further Tomcat's liquor brand. The parties each walked away feeling a bit slighted by the terms, the hallmark of a good compromise.

LVP initially selected CoCo, Inc. ("CoCo"), an upstart manufacturer of spirits who had been on LVP's watch-list for the past few months. CoCo uses a unique coconut nectar recipe to make a fantastic tasting vodka. Because of CoCo's relatively unknown stature, LVP knew they could get CoCo to sign on to manufacture the Tomcat vodka for a great price. LVP pitched the idea to Tomcat, who immediately accepted. LVP subsequently found two other manufacturers for Tomcat over the next 1.5 years, resulting in two additional unique vodka products: Tomcat Ice and Tomcat Nude.

After two years of successful partnership, however, the ideas started to slow down. Tomcat believed that LVP was abusing the exclusive agreement and not working as hard as it should to find Tomcat other avenues in the spirits industry to turn into a profit. Tomcat had introduced no new manufacturing options or other profit earning strategies for a period of six months. During that time, Tomcat was approached by Brogden, a new liquor manufacturer, to make a pumpkin spice vodka. As a result of LVP's lack of work, Tomcat terminated the agreement with LVP without paying LVP the final installment of the license fee. Tomcat also stopped royalty payments for the remaining twelve months of the term. Tomcat entered into a direct agreement with Brogden for the creation of the pumpkin spice vodka. The total net profits for all vodka produced by Tomcat for the last year of the contract was $14 million.

LVP sued Tomcat in state court for breach of contract under Section 45 of Westmoreland law. The parties have agreed to meet to try to settle the matter in lieu of going through the costly pre-trial and trial process.

Westmoreland Civil Code — Section 45

Breach of Contract. A breach of contract shall be determined on a case-by-case basis. An individual or entity that does not complete its obligations under the contract will be found to have breached a contract. An individual or entity can stop performance of their obligations under the contract if the opposing party has already breached the contract. The damages for breach of contract equals the amount of compensation a party would have received had the terms of the contract been fulfilled.

Confidential Facts — Tomcat

Since the termination of the agreement with LVP and news of the lawsuit hit the headlines, Tomcat has been a source of ridicule for the mainstream media. The words "Tomcat" and "corporate greed" have become nearly synonymous. Even before this lawsuit arose, Tomcat was often subject of rumors involving corporate bullying. Tomcat has become infamous within its business circles for telling former business partners, "We have more resources than you do, sue us in court and we'll just stall for years. You'll never see a dime." It is one of the reasons the company has been so profitable under the current Board of Directors.

In the wake of the blowback caused by the termination of the contract with LVP, however, Tomcat's shareholders finally put their foot down. They agreed that they no longer wanted to be associated with a company known for such unethical behavior. Tomcat's shareholders elected to oust the old Chair of the Board and place a new person in charge of LVP's business operations—Nathan Dodge. Mr. Dodge was recently contacted by the CEO of CoCo who informed Mr. Dodge that CoCo will no longer manufacture vodka for Tomcat unless Tomcat is represented by LVP. Given CoCo's coconut vodka brings in 30% of Tomcat's liquor income, Mr. Dodge is worried.

Mr. Dodge wants to clean up Tomcat's corporate image and wants to continue working with CoCo. Settling this lawsuit with LVP is the best place to start on both fronts. Mr. Dodge does not want to lose CoCo as a manufacturer and if working with LVP is the way to get CoCo, he needs you to mend the relationship at these negotiations. Being a highly successful businessperson, however, Mr. Dodge is not willing to give away the farm to LVP. After all, LVP was beginning to slack off and had not made any new deals in the spirits industry on Tomcat's behalf for approximately six months. It is unclear whether LVP's behavior was enough to be considered a breach of the agreement. After all, there may have been limited options during the six months. The deal with Brogden did not turn out as profitable as Tomcat hoped (making only $50,000 net proceeds for the year) and perhaps LVP saw this and chose not to recommend them as a manufacturer. If the judge finds that LVP's behavior does not qualify as a breach, then Tomcat stands to be liable for breaching themselves when Tomcat terminated the agreement.

Tomcat understands that LVP will be asking for the final $3 million installment and royalty payments. Since the company made $14 million net proceeds for vodka in the final year, Tomcat would owe 1.4 million in royalty payments in addition to the $3 million installment. Given that LVP did absolutely no work for the entire second half of the contract (Tomcat did not hear from LVP at all for the 6 months prior to termination and LVP did nothing the final year was after Tomcat terminated the contract), Tomcat is not willing to pay them the full amount. The maximum Mr. Dodge is willing to pay is $3.4 million.

Tomcat would like to continue the relationship with LVP so it can retain CoCo's business. However, the new agreement must (i) be non-exclusive; and (ii) include language that addresses the problems the two companies have faced in the first contract. With respect to exclusivity, Tomcat no longer wants to rely solely on LVP for creative product strategies and wants to leave open the possibility another licensing agency can find deals that LVP cannot. Thus, Tomcat wants the agreement to be non-exclusive. With respect to contractual language, Tomcat wants to be sure there is some incentive to keep LVP working hard for Tomcat. Perhaps the new contract can have language that includes a clause stating that if no new business is generated within a certain period of time, the installment or royalty payments will be decreased by a certain amount. Try to find language that both sides are amenable to.

To convince LVP to sign a new agreement, Mr. Dodge is willing to offer LVP a royalty of up to 25% for all sales resulting from this new agreement. If Tomcat has profits from an idea generated by a different licensing agency, however, LVP will not receive profits from that venture. Tomcat would like the term of the agreement (3 years) and the installment terms (9 million) the same; however, those terms are flexible if needed to get the agreement on the terms stated above.

Above all else, Tomcat wants this lawsuit to go away as quickly as possible. You have discretion to agree to terms requested by LVP as long as they are consistent with Tomcat's interests set forth above. Employ all efforts to ensure that a deal is struck today.

Confidential Facts — LVP

Since the license agreement with Tomcat was terminated, LVP has fallen on hard economic times. The money from the first two installments of the Tomcat agreement was spent long ago, LVP is no longer receiving royalties from Tomcat's vodka, and there is no way LVP can afford to pay for pre-trial and trial expenses. While LVP is considered the best licensing agency of spirits in Westmoreland, their client-base has dried up due to the dominance of a few big brands. There are not very many liquor startups in need of a licensing agency anymore — most just sell their recipes for products directly to established liquor companies.

When Tomcat terminated the agreement with LVP, Tomcat accused LVP of not working to find additional revenue streams in the liquor market. The truth, however, is that LVP was simply unable to find a suitable partner for Tomcat. Most manufacturers were reluctant to get involved with a company of Tomcat's size and reputation. Tomcat has developed quite a reputation for being a dishonest and greedy company. The one company that was interested in Tomcat—Brodgen Liquor—had several failed businesses in the past and Brodgen's pitch about pumpkin spice vodka did not look like a profitable venture. LVP was shocked to hear that Tomcat entered into an agreement with Brodgen and would not be surprised if that relationship was very short lived. LVP has documentation to back up all the work it did to search for revenue streams for Tomcat, but does not have the funds to see this trial to the end—even if LVP would win in court.

By a stroke of good luck, LVP recently stumbled upon a liquor manufacturer named "Rito's." LVP believes that Rito's has come up with a revolutionary vodka recipe that, with the right branding, has the potential to become a nation-wide success. If LVP can get Tomcat to enter into another license agreement, LVP would have the perfect relationship ready to go.

However, LVP is still absolutely incensed at Tomcat for terminating its agreement. LVP wants Tomcat to pay for the damages owed to LVP under the contract. LVP believes it is entitled to 4.2 million total ($3 million for the installment contract and 1.2 million for the 10% royalty). LVP believes it would win the lawsuit if it could afford to go to trial; however, given LVP was unsuccessful in finding additional business for Tomcat and given LVP did not work the last year of the contract after Tomcat terminated it, LVP is willing to settle for $2.2 million.

LVP is in dire financial circumstances and wants to use the lawsuit to get Tomcat to enter into a new license agreement with LVP. LVP already has Rito's on board and ready to go and LVP is certain Rito's idea will be extremely profitable for Tomcat—more so than even the coconut vodka produced by CoCo. Thus, LVP wants any new agreement to include an improved royalty rate. LVP would like 30% of all the sales resulting from the agreement; however, it would be willing to settle for 15% if necessary to get Tomcat to the table.

To ease Tomcat's worries about LVP's "best efforts," LVP is willing to include new language in the agreement that will make Tomcat confident that LVP truly does use its best efforts to find Tomcat business. For example, if Tomcat wants language in the contract that LVP must produce at least one lead every six months or the contract will be terminated or if Tomcat wants documentation regarding its best efforts to be reported regularly, LVP would be willing to do that. You have discretion to agree to language that will put Tomcat's worries at ease, but keep LVP's interests in mind. Regardless of what language is agreed to, however, LVP must retain royalty rights for the remainder of the three-year term for any company introduced to Tomcat by LVP. In other words, if you agree the contract is terminated under certain conditions, LVP will agree to lose any remaining installment payment, but will require that LVP still receives the royalty payment for any company introduced to Tomcat by LVP for the remainder of the term.

You have flexibility to work with the other terms of the agreement. For example, LVP will agree to a non-exclusive agreement if necessary. If Tomcat requests a non-exclusive agreement, LVP wants to be able to monitor the resulting sales received by Tomcat. LVP does not trust Tomcat and wants to be sure that if Tomcat is working with other agencies that LVP is receiving all the profit it is entitled to. LVP would like Tomcat to pay for such an audit as a token of good faith. However, if necessary, LVP will settle for paying for the audit.

LVP is also willing to be flexible with the length of the contract and installment fee. LVP prefers to keep the contract length the same at 3 years and hopes to receive the same installment fee—$9 million, but those numbers are slightly negotiable if necessary to reach a deal. Don't stray too far from the original terms on those issues.

If Tomcat agrees to all of these terms, LVP will drop the lawsuit. You have discretion to agree to terms that are consistent with LVP's interests set forth above. Due to the financial stress on LVP, employ all efforts to ensure that a deal is struck today.

Appendix D

Additional Negotiation Problem: High Difficulty

General Facts
O'Brien v. CSA
By Tim Kuhl

The Collegiate Sports Association, CSA, is a Non-Profit Organization that organizes and regulates all collegiate sports in San Angeles. Composed of 120 colleges and universities, the 120 member schools are divided into three divisions based upon the size of the school and student body, facilities, and school ranking. Division I schools are the largest, Division II schools are mid-sized, and Division III schools are the smallest.

The CSA Committee on Infractions investigates allegations of misconduct or rule violations and may determine that a violation of CSA rules warrants sanctions, probation, or even suspension from a particular sport for the school or the athlete. The most frequent violations the committee investigates are allegations that student-athletes have received compensation in either the form of money or property (aside from any school sponsored scholarships) for their participation in a given sport.

CSA student-athletes are required to sign Form T-10, in which student-athletes agree to receive no compensation as a requirement of their participation in their schools' athletic programs. Form T-10 further grants the CSA permission to use the students' names, images, and likenesses and bars the student-athlete from making use of these publicity rights.

The CSA has a longstanding licensing agreement with Electronic Games, EG, for the highly successful *CSA Football* video game series, which is in its sixth year of production. *CSA Football VI* will be released in February of next year.

The popularity of the video game franchise stems from EG's efforts to make the game as authentic as possible. Featuring the majority of Division I schools, the actual team rosters are used with the real names of the student-athletes and their corresponding team numbers. The majority of the video game avatars are designed using the likenesses of the actual student-athletes. The games provide the user with a realistic experience, which includes players being injured, the ability to substitute players between plays, and the ability to decline or accept penalties. There is also a "Dynasty" mode that allows users to effectively coach their favorite teams through the entire simulated season.

CSA Football IV and *CSA Football V each* grossed over $100 million, and *CSA Football VI is* expected to exceed this amount.

The marketing campaign for the *CSA Football* franchise uses the name and likeness of the player who receives the Most Valuable Player Award, MVP Award, from the Collegiate Championship game. The MVP appears on the cover of the video game, the packaging of the game, and advertising for the game. The advertising campaign includes print advertising in magazines, as well as electronic advertising. Additionally, the MVP films a commercial promoting the video game, which appears on television and the Internet. The winner of the MVP Award from the Collegiate Championship game was Robert O'Brien.

Robert O'Brien accomplished what no other student-athlete has ever achieved: he not only won a third straight Collegiate Championship game, but he received the MVP Award for the third consecutive year. As a result of his first two MVP Awards, O'Brien was featured prominently on the *CSA Football IV* and *CSA Football V* video game covers, packaging, and advertising. He also filmed commercials promoting each game.

As the number one recruit out of High School, O'Brien was highly sought after by the top schools in the CSA and ultimately chose to enroll at San Angeles State University, the defending Collegiate Champions at the time. Beginning his junior year as the

starting quarterback, he led his team to the Collegiate Championship game and won both his first Collegiate Championship and
his first MVP Award. He led his team to victory again during the
next season and chose to return for a fifth year, ultimately winning
a Third Collegiate Championship and MVP award.

Ending last season, O'Brien was considered the number one recruit for the Professional Football League, PFL, and was expected
to have a long career in professional football. Unfortunately, O'Brien
suffered an injury during a ski trip last month. What at first ap-
peared to be only a minor injury, having a minimal impact upon
his expected professional career, was ultimately diagnosed as a career ending spinal injury. While O'Brien has the ability to run and
a full range of motion from his throwing arm, his doctors advised
him that being subjected to the rigors of professional football, such
as being repeatedly tackled, could result in permanent impairment.

Last year, the CSA received a letter from O'Brien's attorneys ad-
vising them that O'Brien would not be filming the commercial promoting *CSA Football VI unless* he was fairly compensated for the
commercial and for the current and past use of his name and likeness on the cover of the video game, packaging, advertising, and
the use of his avatar in the game. Furthermore, the letter stated that
if O'Brien is not fairly compensated, he will file a lawsuit against
the CSA claiming that he was deceived out of just compensation by
being forced to sign Form T-10 in order to play collegiate football.

O'Brien asserts, under the laws of San Angeles, that the CSA has
violated his publicity rights to his own name and likeness, while at
the same time profiting from the use of his name and likeness by
licensing his publicity rights to EG in the form of *CSA Football IV*,
CSA Football V, and the yet to be released *CSA Football VI*.

In response, the CSA stated in a letter to O'Brien that the organization does not license the names or likenesses of student-athletes
to EG, only the CSA name and logo are licensed. This licensing fee
is used to fund CSA operations, staff salaries, and for the betterment
of member schools and student-athletes. Furthermore, Form T-10
is designed to protect student-athletes from exploitation, as well as
to allow member schools the ability to maintain control over their
athletic departments.

Both parties have agreed to enter into good-faith negotiations to discuss these issues and work toward an amicable conclusion, if possible.

Applicable San Angeles Law

San Angeles Civil Code § 10: Definitions:

The term "person" as used in the Civil Code includes both individuals and all business entities or companies.

San Angeles Civil Code § 3344: Right of Publicity

(a) Any person who knowingly uses another's name, voice, image, or likeness, in any manner, on or in products, merchandise, or goods, or for purposes of advertising or selling, without such person's prior consent, shall be liable for any damages sustained by the person or persons injured as a result thereof.

(b) The person who violated the section shall be liable to the injured party or parties for the actual damages suffered by him or her as a result of the unauthorized use, and any profits from the unauthorized use that are attributable to the use. Punitive damages may also be awarded to the injured party or parties. The prevailing party in any action under this section shall also be entitled to attorney's fees and costs.

San Angles Civil Code § 128: Undue Influence

If a person enters into an agreement with another by taking advantage of a special or particularly persuasive relationship that the person shares with the other, a court can find the resulting agreement unenforceable on grounds of undue influence. In determining whether the agreement is unenforceable, the court will consider the totality of the circumstances.

San Angles Civil Code § 129: Unconscionability

Unconscionability means that a term in the contract or something inherent in or about the agreement was so shockingly unfair that the contract simply cannot be allowed to stand as is. In determining whether a contract is void for unconscionability, the court will consider:

- whether one side has grossly unequal bargaining power
- whether one side had difficulty understanding the terms of the agreement (due to language or literacy issues, for example), or
- whether the terms themselves were unfair.

If a court does find a contract unconscionable, it has options other than just voiding the agreement altogether. It may instead choose to enforce the conscionable parts of the contract and rewrite the unconscionable term or clause.

Confidential Facts — Robert O'Brien

Robert O'Brien's career ending injury has profoundly affected his personal life and has thrown his professional future into uncertainty. He expected to graduate the number-one overall draft pick for the Professional Football League and sign a multi-million-dollar contract with a top team. Instead, he is facing the fact his dream to play professional football ended before he ever stepped foot on the field. His once certain future earning potential has turned into an uncertain financial future.

Even before his injury, Rob had expressed his displeasure with the CSA's Form T-10. He always believed that forcing all student-athletes to sign the form as a condition to play collegiate sports was both unfair and designed to ensure that the CSA and its member schools could freely profit from student-athletes' blood and sweat. It is almost impossible for someone to be signed to a professional sport without first attending an undergraduate institution, and all undergraduate institutions are member schools of the CSA. Rob has witnessed several of his fellow players and friends suffer terrible injuries during televised sporting events, which they received no compensation for, while the school made a profit from ticket sales, and the CSA profited from advertising revenue and media rights contracts.

Looking back on his collegiate career, Rob feels justified that he is duly owed compensation given his accomplishments on and off the field. San Angeles State University made millions, if not tens of millions, from the three Collegiate Championship victories to which he led his team. The CSA and EG have made hundreds of millions of dollars from the *CSA Football* franchise, using his name and likeness on the game covers, packaging, and advertising, as well as his promotion of the games in television and Internet commercials.

Regardless of whether the CSA's claim that is does not license student-athletes' names and likenesses to EG bears any merit, the CSA uses Form T-10 in conjunction with its policy of prohibiting student-athletes from receiving compensation to effectively deny student-athletes from exercising their right of publicity.

Rob's situation is a perfect example of injury to the right of publicity the CSA is promulgating. It is egregious that the CSA prevents him from entering into a licensing agreement with EG for the use of his own name and likeness as an avatar in a video game and prominence on the game cover, packaging, and promotional advertising. Further, it is an overreach of CSA authority to deny him the ability to receive compensation for appearing in a commercial promoting the video game after he has graduated and is no longer a student-athlete.

While Rob is willing to file a lawsuit against the CSA and litigate his legal claims, his primary concern is ensuring his financial security. In moving forward with this negotiation, Rob would prefer to reach an agreement with the CSA so long as it provides for both his immediate and future financial needs. Ultimately, Rob will only forgo filing a lawsuit if he is fairly compensated for the use of his name and likeness in conjunction with the *CSA Football* franchise. This includes the use of his avatar, his name and likeness on the game cover, packaging, and advertising, along with filming any commercials promoting the sixth version of the video game.

Compensation for Name and Likeness

Rob considers $3 million to be fair compensation for the use of his name and likeness; $1 million for each year the CSA and EG exploited his right of publicity. Rob feels that this is a reasonable figure as it represents only 1% of the gross proceeds each *CSA Football* video game earned or is expected to earn. Rob is willing to accept as little as $2 million if necessary to reach agreement.

Compensation for Commercial Promoting Version VI of the Video Game

Rob also believes that he deserves at least an additional $250,000 to film the commercial promoting the sixth version of the video game. Rob is not requesting any compensation for the previous two commercials he filmed, as those commercials increased his national exposure and furthered his goal of playing in the PFL. However, he is no longer going to play in the PFL and is no longer a student. He will only film the commercial if he is compensated and wants at least $250,000 for his time.

Additional Commercials/Promotions

Rob will agree to additional promotional commercials or other forms of promotion for the sixth version of the video game on the condition that he is paid at least $100,000 per promotional event or promotional commercial and/or a total of $500,000 for all events/commercials. Rob is very willing to participate in additional commercials and events, as he greatly enjoys the fame and attention, and those days will soon be behind him. Rob would like to participate in as many commercials and events as possible, as long as his minimum price is agreed to.

Confidentiality

If the CSA insists upon any form of a confidentiality clause regarding the nature and/or terms of the agreement, Rob will need at least an additional $500,000 in compensation. Rob would prefer not to agree to any form of a confidentiality clause, as he feels the CSA is unlawfully depriving thousands of student-athletes their right of publicity, but understands this is a common contractual term.

So long as the agreement with the CSA adheres to the aforementioned conditions and compensation amounts, Rob is willing to accept any reasonable request or condition made by the CSA. Rob will also agree to accept a single monetary amount that encompasses all of the above-mentioned categories: past and present use of his name and likeness, promotional commercial for the fifth version of the game, other promotional events, and any form of a confidentiality clause.

Confidential Facts—Collegiate Sports Association

The CSA maintains that Mr. O'Brien's claims are without merit, and Form T-10 is essential to maintain order in collegiate sports. The licensing agreement with EA pertains only to the name and logo of the CSA to be used in the video game itself, as well as on the cover, packaging, and advertising. The licensing fee the CSA received from EG for the fourth, fifth, and sixth versions of the game were each $5 million, a fraction of the total value of the franchise. Mr. O'Brien's claim that the CSA "profits" from this licensing agreement is both malicious and inaccurate.

As an NPO, the CSA uses this licensing fee to pay for the daily operation of the organization, staff salaries, and for the betterment of member schools and their student-athletes. Any surplus revenue received is maintained in an account to cover unexpected expenses, such as legal fees and litigation expenses. Furthermore, the CSA does not license the names and likenesses of student-athletes and certainly does not "profit" by it. At most, CSA policies prevent student-athletes from licensing their names and likenesses or from entering into licensing arrangements. These policies are necessary, however, and are reasonable given the structure of collegiate sports.

All member schools in the CSA are free to enter into licensing agreements for their athletic departments, and all Division I and Division II schools have such agreements in place. These range from licensing agreements for team uniforms, athletic equipment, and merchandise to the beverages served on the sidelines. Member schools are thorough in offsetting their expenses with these licensing agreements, and the competition among sports apparel companies can be fierce. It is common practice for a school to enter into an agreement with a company that sells sports apparel and footwear to supply the school's athletic department with team uniforms. In return, the company's logo or brand name is featured on the uniform, and the company enters into a merchandising agreement to sell team jerseys and other merchandise in their stores.

If student-athletes were free to enter into licensing agreements for their names and likenesses with sports apparel companies, it would create an inherent conflict between the schools' licensing and merchandising agreements and the student-athlete. All members of a collegiate football team could have their own individual licensing agreements with rival companies to that of their school. This would prevent schools from controlling their own athletic departments, which is why after due research and consideration the Board of Directors voted to enact Form T-10 and other policies preventing student-athletes from exercising their right of publicity while receiving their education.

Although the CSA is confident in its position regarding student-athlete right of publicity, this specific situation with Mr. O'Brien presents a unique set of circumstances. Unlike the merchandising agreements member schools enter into with different companies, the video game rights would not cause a conflict among schools. Featuring Mr. O'Brien's name and likeness so prominently on the video game cover, packaging, and advertising without compensation could be harder to justify and further sets his claim against the CSA apart from other student-athletes.

The CSA's primary concern with a potential lawsuit from Mr. O'Brien is that other collegiate student-athletes, both ex-players and current, may see this as an opportunity to file lawsuits of their own. This could result in thousands, if not tens of thousands, of lawsuits filed against the CSA, or, worse, an attempt to bring all these claims under a single class action lawsuit. Any player whose name and likeness were used in any of the *CSA Football* video games could be a potential plaintiff. Resolving this dispute with Mr. O'Brien before a lawsuit is filed is of the upmost concern of the CSA, as well as handling this situation a quietly as possible.

If this negotiation does not conclude in a manner that prevents a lawsuit from being filed and in a manner that maintains the confidential nature and terms of the agreement, the CSA may be forced to end its licensing agreement with EG, making *CSA Football VI* the final installment of the video game. As CSA is a Non-Profit Organization, the licensing agreement with EG provides essential funding to the CSA. Thus, the CSA is willing to be flexible in working with Mr. O'Brien to resolve this dispute.

Confidentiality Clause

An essential term of any agreement with Mr. O'Brien is that he agrees to a confidentiality clause as to the nature of this negotiation, as well as the terms agreed upon. Mr. O'Brien will be compensated up to $1 million in order to achieve his silence; however the CSA is not willing to settle without his agreement to keep the agreement confidential.

Compensation for Name and Likeness in Promotional Material and Commercials

It is important that the release of *CSA Football VI* follows the precedent established by the other five versions of the game. Thus, the CSA must have Mr. O'Brien agree to film a promotional commercial for *CSA Football VI*. To ensure this commercial is filmed, the CSA is willing to compensate Mr. O'Brien for the past use of his name and likeness in all video game covers, packaging, advertising, and commercials filmed. The CSA is willing to pay up to $3 million in total for versions IV, V, and VI of the video game. This is a fair amount as it is nearly one-third of what the CSA received as a license fee from EG for all three seasons of the video game.

The CSA would like you to be clear, however, exactly what the compensation is for. The amount agreed upon for the use of his name and likeness is only for the use of his name and likeness in conjunction with the video game cover, packaging, advertising, and commercials filmed. The CSA is not willing to compensate Mr. O'Brien at all for the use of his name/likeness in connection with his avatar in the game. It must be absolutely clear that the payment from the CSA is only for the promotional material (cover, packaging, commercial, etc.) and not for the use of his likeness in creating his avatar used in the game. The CSA cannot allow any precedent to be set for compensating student-athletes for the use of their names and likenesses in their video game avatars. This would open the CSA to future litigation from any former or current student-athlete whose name and likeness were used as avatars in any of the video games' six versions. Limiting compensation to only the video game cover, packaging, and advertising limits potential plaintiffs to the three other MVP award winners, each of whom have multi-million dollar contracts with NFL teams and are unlikely to file a lawsuit against the CSA.

Thus, in order to award Mr. O'Brien any funds for the use of his name and likeness, you must make clear exactly what he is being compensated for and Mr. O'Brien must waive any future claims related to the use of his name and likeness. The waiver must include a provision that Mr. O'Brien is waiving all claims relating to the use of his avatar.

Additional Promotional Commercials

The CSA would also like Mr. O'Brien film additional promotional commercials and attend additional promotional events in order to offer a public explanation for this CSA-O'Brien negotiation.

First, the CSA would like Mr. O'Brien to agree to a joint press release prepared by the CSA announcing the successful completion of negotiations between the parties. The CSA will pay O'Brien $100,000 for his cooperation in the press release.

The CSA will also compensate Mr. O'Brien up to $750,000 for his participation in three additional promotional commercials (although four commercials would be preferred).

In addition, Mr. O'Brien will be compensated up to $700,000, in total, to participate in six promotional events for the video game (although his participation in eight would be ideal). Four of these events will be the four largest video game conferences in the country, held in January of next year. The fifth event will be the February 1st release date for the video game (next year). The sixth event will be the Collegiate Championship game, held in January of next year. The two additional events are still in the planning stages, but will be held in late March or early April of next year.

Appendix E

Example Score Sheet

Competitor's Name: _____   Judge's Name: _____

SCORE	CLASSIFICATION
1	Exceptional
2	Great
3	Good
4	Average
5	Needs improvement
6	Needs significant improvement

CATEGORIES: (Please give a score 1–6 in each category on the line provided)

_____ A. PREPARATION/ STRATEGY

In the "preparation—negotiation strategy and tactics" category, the judges will assess how well the team prepared for the negotiation given the time permitted, whether the strategy fit the facts, the law, and the client's objectives; whether the team anticipated the strategy and tactics of the opposing team; and whether the team thought of creative approaches to the negotiation.

_____ B. EXECUTION/ OUTCOME

In the "execution/ outcome of the negotiation" category, the judges will assess how well the final outcome of the negotiation advances the interests of the team's client. Inflexible and stubborn conduct should receive low scores. The execution of strategy, adaptability, flexibility, and creativity will be assessed.

____ C. TEAMWORK
In the "teamwork" category the judges will assess how well the team worked together in executing its strategy, as well as how the team interacted with the other team in trying to facilitate an agreement. In particular, the score in this category should reflect whether the team was able to jointly adapt and react to new information and unexpected moves by the other side. The scores should also reflect how effective the team members were in sharing responsibility, backing each other up, and not undercutting each other.

____ D. OVERALL ABILITY
In the "overall ability" category judges will evaluate basic oral presentation skills and basic teachability. The "oral presentation" of the applicant should possess the requisite articulateness, clarity, persuasiveness, and effectiveness. The presentation should also be professional.

____ E. SELF EVALUATION
In the self-evaluation category, judges will evaluation the student's assessment of the negotiation. The students have been asked to address (i) how their strategy worked with respect to the ultimate outcome and (ii) what they would change about the negotiation and what they would keep the same.

Total Score: _____ (5 is the best total score a student can receive)

Comments: _____

_____

_____

_____

Appendix F

Answer Key to Quizzes

Chapter 1

1. C
2. Pro: Ice-breaking gives the parties a chance to relax and ice-breaking is consistent with real-world negotiations.
   Con: If the opposing side takes the table, the judges may perceive them as taking control of the negotiation.
3. False
4. False
5. D

Chapter 2

1. False
2. A and B
3. False
4. B
5. True

Chapter 3

1. False
2. True
3. D
4. A
5. False

Chapter 4

1. False
2. A
3. False
4. True
5. End your introduction with an information gathering question.

Chapter 5

1. True
2. B
3. True
4. True
5. A

Chapter 6

1. False
2. D
3. Black
4. False
5. C

Chapter 7

1. False
2. True
3. Clear, Reasonable, Fair
4. False
5. True

Chapter 8

1. False
2. True
3. D
4. A
5. C

Chapter 9

1. D
2. False
3. D
4. True
5. False

Chapter 10

1. False
2. A and D
3. False
4. D
5. False

Chapter 11

1. False
2. Skirt below knee; closed-toe pump; clothes that fit; no beard; black suit
3. Never
4. False
5. False

Chapter 12

1. True
2. True
3. False
4. False
5. C and D

Appendix G

Southwestern Law School Competition Victories

2008
Champions—ABA Regional Negotiation Competition
Third Place—ABA Regional Client Counseling Competition

2009
Champions—International BLSA Competition
Champions—ABA Regional Arbitration Competition
Second Place—ABA Client Counseling Competition
Fourth Place—ABA Regional Negotiation Competition

2010
Champions—International BLSA Negotiation Competition
Second Place—Richmond National Environmental Negotiation
    Competition

2011
Champions—International BLSA Negotiation Competition
Champions—Thomas Jefferson's National Sports Law Negotiation
    Competition
Champions—Lewis & Clark School of Law National Environmental
    Negotiation Competition
Second Place—Liberty University School of Law Negotiation Competition
Second Place—California Bar Association Environmental Negotiation Competition
Third Place—Lewis & Clark School of Law National Environmental
    Negotiation Competition

Third Place—Thomas Jefferson's National Sports Law Negotiation Competition

Fourth Place—Liberty University School of Law Negotiation Competition

2012

Champions—ABA Regional Negotiation Competition

Champions—International BLSA Negotiation Competition

Champions—Liberty University School of Law Negotiation Competition

Champions—Lewis & Clark School of Law National Environmental Negotiation Competition

Second Place—Lewis & Clark School of Law National Environmental Negotiation Competition

Second Place—Thomas Jefferson's National Sports Law Negotiation Competition

Third Place—Liberty University School of Law Negotiation Competition

2013

Fourth Place—Lewis & Clark School of Law National Environmental Negotiation Competition

2014

Champions—ABA Regional Representation in Mediation Competition

Champions—ABA Regional Client Counseling Competition

Second Place—ABA Regional Negotiation Competition

Third Place—Thomas Jefferson's National Sports Law Negotiation Competition

Fourth Place—Liberty University School of Law Negotiation Competition

Sixth Place—ABA National Client Counseling Competition

2015

Champions—ABA Regional Representation in Mediation Competition

Champions—Thomas Jefferson's National Sports Law Negotiation Competition

Second Place—ABA National Representation in Mediation Competition

Second Place—California Bar Association Environmental Negotiation Competition

Second Place—Liberty University School of Law Negotiation Competition

Fifth Place—ABA National Negotiation Competition

Semi-Finalist—International Academy of Dispute Resolution Mediation Competition

2016

Second Place—ABA Regional Negotiation Competition

Second Place—Liberty University School of Law Negotiation Competition

Third Place—William and Mary International Law National Negotiation Competition

2017

Champions—ABA National Representation in Mediation Competition

Champions—ABA Regional Representation in Mediation Competition

Second Place—Fordham University School of Law's National NBA Basketball Negotiation Competition

Third Place—ABA Regional Representation in Mediation Competition

Index